Classroom Assessment for Teachers

This accessible guide shows just how straightforward it can be to create excellent classroom assessment for formative or summative purposes, giving you confidence in your assessment practices.

It clearly sets out the principles underpinning all good educational assessment and translates them into a series of practical steps. These can be put into practice in a wide range of classroom contexts to fit the purposes of every teacher. Written by two assessment specialists with decades of experience in the UK and internationally, this readable and well-structured text encourages teachers to examine assumptions and challenge the use of assessment that is not fit for purpose. Including summaries of key ideas, questions and takeaways, chapters cover

- The purposes of educational assessment
- Understanding what you want to assess
- How to get the evidence you need
- Assessment design
- The outcomes of assessment and providing feedback

Designed to inspire and support teachers and teachers-in-training across both primary and secondary phases, this book is a valuable resource for creating the kinds of assessment that will benefit learners in the ways that all good assessment should.

Lena Gray has extensive experience of developing assessment policies, supporting teachers and examiners in the implementation of these, and evaluating assessment policy and practice. She was formerly Director of Research and Analysis at AQA, England's largest GCSE and A-level exam board.

Lesley Wiseman-Orr is a research fellow in the School of Education at the University of Glasgow, Scotland. She sits on the Council of the Association for Educational Assessment Europe. She is also a member of the International Educational Assessment Network, which brings experts together to share evidence from research and practice, generate new ideas and address common problems in educational assessment.

Classroom Assessment for Teachers

Turning Principles into Practice

Lena Gray and Lesley Wiseman-Orr

LONDON AND NEW YORK

Designed cover image: © Getty Images

First published 2026
by Routledge
4 Park Square, Milton Park, Abingdon, Oxon OX14 4RN

and by Routledge
605 Third Avenue, New York, NY 10158

Routledge is an imprint of the Taylor & Francis Group, an informa business

© 2026 Lena Gray and Lesley Wiseman-Orr

The right of Lena Gray and Lesley Wiseman-Orr to be identified as authors of this work has been asserted in accordance with sections 77 and 78 of the Copyright, Designs and Patents Act 1988.

All rights reserved. No part of this book may be reprinted or reproduced or utilised in any form or by any electronic, mechanical, or other means, now known or hereafter invented, including photocopying and recording, or in any information storage or retrieval system, without permission in writing from the publishers.

Trademark notice: Product or corporate names may be trademarks or registered trademarks, and are used only for identification and explanation without intent to infringe.

British Library Cataloguing-in-Publication Data
A catalogue record for this book is available from the British Library

ISBN: 978-1-032-91696-5 (hbk)
ISBN: 978-1-032-91695-8 (pbk)
ISBN: 978-1-003-56447-8 (ebk)

DOI: 10.4324/9781003564478

Typeset in Celeste and Optima
by Apex CoVantage, LLC

Access the Support Material: www.routledge.com/9781032916958

Contents

	Preface	x
	Introduction	1

Section 1: Educational assessment and the principles that underpin it   5

1   Educational assessment and the role of the teacher   7

The value of measurement and assessment	7
The development of educational assessment	8
Assessment, curriculum and pedagogy	10
Educational assessment as the judging of evidence of learning	11
Educational assessment: purpose and consequences, timing, frequency and formality	13
The role of the teacher in externally devised assessment	15
Teacher-devised classroom assessment	16
Summary	20

2   The qualities of all good educational assessment: Validity, reliability, fairness and practicality   21

Validity	22
Validity and assessment purpose	23
Devising valid assessment	24

Contents

	Reliability	25
	The relationship between reliability and validity	27
	Reliability and assessment purpose	27
	Fairness	28
	Fairness in educational assessment	28
	Relationships between fairness, reliability and validity	29
	Fair assessment is good for everyone	31
	Practicality	32
	Relationships between practicality and fairness, reliability and validity	33
	Practicality and assessment purpose	34
	Getting the balance right for assessment that is fit for purpose	35
	Summary	35
3	The ethics of educational assessment	37
	What kinds of good can educational assessment do?	38
	What kinds of harm can educational assessment do?	39
	The ethics of educational assessment	40
	Summary	42

Section 2: Practical steps for devising good assessment in the classroom — 43

4	Be clear about why you want to assess	45
	Assessment purpose informs everything	46
	Purposes of classroom assessment	47
	Assessment for learning	48
	Assessment of learning	51
	Diagnostic assessment	55
	Summary	56
5	Be clear about who you want to assess	58
	Think of your students	58
	Make sure your assessment is for all of your students	59
	Summary	61

Contents

6	Be clear about what you want to assess	62
	The focus of assessment	63
	Intended learning outcomes	64
	Action verbs	*65*
	Assessment of abstract constructs	66
	Share your assessment focus with your students	69
	Summary	70
7	Choose approaches and methods to suit your purpose and the evidence for assessment you need	72
	Evidence for assessment should be relevant and adequate	73
	Gathering evidence for assessment	74
	Generating evidence for assessment	75
	Methods of assessment	76
	Using more than one method of assessment	79
	Authentic assessment	79
	Tests and exams	80
	What's good about tests and exams?	*81*
	What's the problem with tests and exams?	*83*
	All assessment methods have strengths and weaknesses	84
	Summary	85
8	Create assessment tasks that help students produce the evidence for assessment you need	86
	A test worth teaching to	87
	Different kinds of assessment task or item	87
	Assessment items with a correct answer	*88*
	Items intended to elicit a range of acceptable responses or evidence of particular kinds	*91*
	Communication and common problems with assessment tasks	93
	Communication	*94*
	Command verbs	*94*
	Using context in assessment tasks and items	*95*
	Using illustrations in assessment tasks and items	*97*

Contents

	Including optional tasks or items in your assessment	98
	Including scaffolding or stages in your assessment task or items	99
	Avoiding assessment drift	100
	Assessment context and conditions of assessment	101
	Assessment context	101
	Conditions of assessment	102
	Efficiency in assessment	104
	Summary	105
9	Judging evidence for assessment	106
	The importance of alignment	106
	Instructions to self!	109
	Students should know how their evidence will be judged	110
	Approaches to marking or judging evidence for assessment	110
	Allocating marks to different parts of an assessment	116
	Turning marks into grades	117
	The critical importance of communication	118
	Quality assurance	119
	Summary	120
10	Making good use of the outcomes of assessment	121
	Using assessment outcomes according to assessment purpose	121
	Forms of assessment outcomes	122
	Assessment outcomes fit for assessment purposes	124
	Using assessment outcomes for formative purposes	125
	Using assessment outcomes for summative purposes	128
	Using assessment outcomes for diagnostic purposes	129
	Communicating assessment outcomes beyond the classroom	129
	Summary	132

Contents

11 Overview of the principles of assessment and practical
    steps for putting these into practice   133

Chapter 4: Be clear about why you want to assess   135
Chapter 5: Be clear about who you want to assess   135
Chapter 6: Be clear about what you want to assess   136
Chapter 7: Choose approaches and methods to suit your
    purpose and the evidence for assessment you need   136
Chapter 8: Create assessment tasks that help students
    produce the evidence for assessment you need   137
Chapter 9: Judging evidence for assessment   137
Chapter 10: Making good use of the outcomes of
    assessment   138
Appendix 1 The importance of alignment   139

Glossary   140
Index   144

Preface

We assume you have picked up this book because you are interested in assessment. Or perhaps you are more generally interested in education and have concerns about the role of assessment in that. You may be a teacher or a student teacher. Perhaps you are a student who is preparing for an important assessment. Or you have responsibility for devising or delivering assessment. Whoever you are, we assume that assessment feels important to you. And you'd be right. Good educational assessment offers great benefits to students and others. But educational assessment also carries some risks, especially when it is not fit for purpose. We hope this little book will help you to avoid those risks. We intend it to offer clear ideas about why good assessment is important and how to create it.

This is not an 'academic' textbook, but its content is informed by internationally recognised good practice: what has been shown to work. It is also informed by the conversations we have had with teachers and other assessment professionals over many years, in our diverse roles that include researcher, teacher, policymaker and assessment developer. These conversations convinced us of the potential value to teachers and teachers in training of a small book that conveys some fairly fundamental 'rules' for creating good educational assessment in a way that everyone can understand, remember and be able to put into practice whenever they need to. We sincerely hope that this is

Preface

what you will find in our little book. Our focus will be on the kinds of educational assessment that you can create in your classroom and that will allow your students to best show you what they know and can do.

We hope you will find what follows to be accessible, informative and interesting. It may offer you a perspective on educational assessment that allows you to more easily think beyond the traditional approaches with which you might be most familiar. We certainly hope that its basis in underlying principles will give you a deeper understanding of educational assessment. One that will allow you to critically evaluate different kinds of assessment you may have used in the past or may want to use in the future. Most of all, we hope it will give you the confidence to devise great assessment for your own students.

Introduction

Educational assessment is important to us as individuals and collectively. Good educational assessment can provide us with important opportunities to show what we know and can do. It can motivate and reward us. As a society, we can have confidence in what good educational assessment tells us and use that to make decisions of many different kinds. But poorly devised educational assessment can fail to provide those benefits and can sometimes cause harms instead, especially to learning and to learner wellbeing.

While most would include assessment of teachers, schools and even education systems as forms of educational assessment, in this book, we are focused on the most common use – the assessment of students in the classroom and the uses to which its outcomes, whatever form those may take, are put. Some of that assessment is provided by others, and we will touch on that, but in this book, our focus will be teacher-devised assessment.

Teacher-devised assessment may take a little time to create, but the process can be highly rewarding when you understand and are able to focus on what's important and, thus, can have positive impacts on the students in your classroom. We hope that understanding what's important for teacher-devised assessment will bring to life those principles that should underpin all good educational assessment.

Classroom Assessment for Teachers

To a very large extent, the principles underpinning good educational assessment are universally applicable to high-quality assessment and measurement of all kinds. We are attempting in this small book to communicate those principles as clearly as possible and show how they can inform assessment practice. Educational assessment is not 'rocket science', but it takes some effort to do well. It's worth that effort . . . and it gets easier with practice!

In Section 1 of this book, we explain why it's important to get educational assessment right, and the principles that underpin all good educational assessment. In the second section, we show how these principles can be translated into practical steps for anyone devising good assessment. These practical steps are designed to answer questions you may already have asked yourself or ones we'd recommend you do: Why do you want to assess? Who do you want to assess? What do you want to assess? How do you begin to create good assessment? How do you get the details right? How should evidence for assessment be judged? How should you use the outcomes of assessment?

In the course of this book, we will try to answer each of these questions. We will carefully structure and signpost the text through headings and sub-headings and through highlighting key ideas to create a text that you can scan and dip into and return to at any time. These signposts should help to guide you through the thinking behind good assessment as well as the process of creating it. You will find that process summarised in Chapter 11.

We have tried to write this book using plain language, avoiding as far as possible some of the 'technical' terms that can make any subject seem inaccessible and exclusive. Sometimes, though, it can be helpful to know a more technical term because it has an important meaning that might be different from the more common use of that word. Or such a term might be very useful shorthand. Once you can see how this language of assessment relates to your own practice, we hope that you will become more confident in using it and in communicating with

Introduction

other assessment professionals. When we want to use such a term, we will explain it at first use and, for easy reference, it is included in a glossary at the end of the book.

In the rest of this book, we have chosen to use the term 'student' to mean anyone being assessed, whether that is a pupil in school, a student in college or university, or someone participating in some kind of work-based or job-related training. Similarly, we have chosen to use the word 'teacher' to describe anyone delivering or facilitating a course of learning, whether that is in school, college, university, training organisation or place of work. We have called that place a 'classroom' wherever it happens to be. Sometimes the teacher is also the assessor but not always: when that is the case, we use the word 'assessor' to distinguish these two roles. We mainly use the term 'outcomes' of assessment to describe whatever is available for use at the end of the process of assessment, whatever form that takes, such as written or verbal comments, marks or grades. We will sometimes use the term 'results' where that is commonly used for the outcomes of particular kinds of assessment.

When we talk about teacher-devised assessment, we include in that process all of the decisions and resulting actions that determine the who, when, what and how of classroom assessment. Teacher-devised assessment might be the teacher looking for evidence for assessment during learning or creating a task to generate evidence for assessment. Judging that evidence might result in immediate feedback to a student or in a record or report on what a student has achieved over the course of a period of learning.

This book is all about applying the principles underpinning all good educational assessment. They are as applicable to assessment using virtual reality as they are to assessment using pencil and paper. We introduce those principles in Section 1 of the book, and in Section 2, we translate these into practical steps to help you to devise good assessment for your students. We hope that if we are able to explain well

Classroom Assessment for Teachers

these principles and related practical steps you will look forward to using them to devise all kinds of educational assessment that is very worthwhile for your students and satisfying for you!

Finally, it is important to say that there is much more to be learned and argued than we have chosen to include in this little book. Our aim has been to provide just enough information and explanation to support you to devise good educational assessment. You may not need to know more than this, but you might like to! If that's the case, we hope that this guide will provide you with a range of jumping off points from which you can take a deeper dive into the ideas that most interest you. There's a lot going on in the world of educational assessment, as researchers and theorists explore assessment issues and seek solutions to these. We will be delighted if this little book helps you to engage in those discussions and developments and look forward to seeing you there!

Section 1: Educational assessment and the principles that underpin it

Educational assessment and the role of the teacher

This chapter is all about

- The value of measurement and assessment
- How educational assessment has developed over time
- Assessment, curriculum and pedagogy
- Assessment as the judging of evidence of learning
- Assessment purpose and consequences, timing, frequency and formality
- The role of the teacher in externally devised assessment
- Teacher-devised classroom assessment

The value of measurement and assessment

Assessment is a valuable, indeed essential, activity in everyday life. Assessment is a way of finding out something useful about something or someone and having confidence in that information. In many fields other than education, the more commonly used term for this activity is 'measurement'.

In everyday life, we are generally comfortable with the idea of measurement. We regularly make use of a range of measurement instruments that we routinely depend upon. We use them to measure things like length (with rulers, tape rules or more sophisticated laser instruments) and weight (using different kinds of weighing scales for measuring ingredients in the kitchen and people in the home or at the doctor's surgery).

Even without an instrument, we make assessments all the time and base small and big decisions upon these. Does this taste good? How is my friend feeling? Am I enjoying this class? We are familiar with these processes of measurement and assessment and know how important they are to our lives.

In education, 'assessment' is a more familiar term than 'measurement'. Some are uncomfortable about using the term 'measurement' in education, so we will stick to the word 'assessment' in this book. But the concepts are very similar and the importance is just the same. With good educational assessment, we can find out important things about our students, and that makes educational assessment a very valuable tool.

> You can use good educational assessment to obtain information about your students and to have confidence in that information.

On the other hand, poorly devised assessment won't give us that important information and can also cause harm. The benefits and risks of educational assessment, and the importance of maximising one and minimising the other, are the focus of an early chapter in this book.

The development of educational assessment

The word 'assessment' comes from the Latin 'assidere', which means 'to sit beside'. That's quite a helpful idea. As teachers, we sit beside our students, questioning them, engaging them in discussion, watching them do things, or looking at things they have produced during learning or in response to an assessment task. In all of these situations, we are assessing our students.

Educational assessment and the role of the teacher

Using assessments to work out students' strengths, weaknesses and readiness for next steps began more than a thousand years ago, with the first selection examinations for the Chinese civil service. That approach started to be copied in other countries about 400 years ago, and in the past 150 years, it has become dominant around the world. As a result, when many people think about educational assessment, they immediately picture young people sitting at rows of desks, each with only a set of questions, paper for answers, and something to write those answers with. The room will be quiet except for the scratching of pen on paper. That traditional image of educational assessment – of silent exam halls filled with nervous students and an assessment that some will likely fail, which may endure in your part of the world – is a very old one and feels increasingly out of date. To what extent does this mirror your own experience of educational assessment?

While a test, quiz or exam can often be the most direct and efficient way to assess whether students can remember and use a body of knowledge, nowadays educational assessment can be of many other kinds. Some assessment has much less – or no – requirement for any writing to be done. These might be practical, professional, work-based or competence-based assessments, such as piano exams, driving tests, assessments for doctors and nurses, firefighters and farmers, baristas and ballroom dancers, of swimming and saving swimmers from drowning. For assessment of many kinds of skills and applied knowledge, a written exam would make no sense at all.

We now recognise that it can be good to allow the use of tools and resources during some assessments, like a calculator in a mathematics exam, a book of formulae during a physics exam or a manufacturer's handbook when assessing the installation of a central heating boiler. We understand that working with other students during assessment is not necessarily 'cheating' and might actually create much more authentic assessment. Indeed, some skills can only be assessed in a group situation.

Classroom Assessment for Teachers

In well-resourced classrooms, we might have access to assessment on computers or other digital devices, which can make use of sound, images and simulations and can allow students to hear questions or speak their answers instead of reading them or writing them down. Digital assessments can commonly be tailored to individual students. With new generations of AI, the rapid pace of change in educational assessment is only going to accelerate. The same principles that underpin good educational assessment currently should still underpin good educational assessment in the future.

Assessment, curriculum and pedagogy

Any approach to assessment should be suitable for the curriculum that it supports and the pedagogy that it informs. Many of us are most familiar with a curriculum that is based upon specifying content to be learned or end points to be reached. This book should be very helpful for teachers delivering those kinds of curricula. A curriculum that is more focused on the process than the products of learning is usually not driven by defined and explicit intended learning outcomes. Any approach to assessment for this kind of curriculum will likely need to include a more dynamic and responsive gathering and judging of evidence. Of course, your own curriculum might not be very tightly aligned to any particular approach or may be in the process of moving from one approach towards another! Whatever your approach to curriculum, we would argue that the principles that underpin good educational assessment are applicable to all kinds of measurement or assessment.

> Any approach to assessment should be thoughtfully aligned with curriculum and pedagogy.

Educational assessment as the judging of evidence of learning

Whatever the curriculum and its related approach to assessment, educational assessment is a process that involves the judging of evidence of learning and using the outcomes of that in a purposeful way. Notice that the process of assessment doesn't end with generating assessment outcomes, such as commentary, marks or grades. It ends with the ways in which those assessment outcomes are used.

> Educational assessment is a process that involves the judging of evidence of learning and using the outcomes of that activity in a purposeful way.

There are many ways to obtain evidence for assessment, but these fall into two broad categories. Evidence for assessment can be produced naturally in the course of learning or it can be deliberately generated using some kind of assessment task.

Evidence for assessment can be something tangible – something we can touch that is produced by students in the course of their learning or in response to an assessment task. For example, a piece of art, a calculation, an essay, a cake, a dissertation or a wall. Or evidence can be ephemeral – something that cannot be touched but can be observed. That could be the performance of a skill – dancing, joinery, customer service – or demonstration of knowledge evidenced during discussion with an assessor.

> Evidence for assessment can be tangible or intangible, gathered naturally in the course of learning or generated using an assessment task of some kind.

Classroom Assessment for Teachers

An assessment task intended to generate tangible or ephemeral evidence for assessment might be a test, quiz or exam; a written brief for making a wedding cake, preparing a report or carrying out an experiment; or verbal instructions for performing a piece of music, a driving manoeuvre or walking along a beam. There are many kinds of evidence for assessment, and these can be obtained in many different ways, but the same principles of assessment should underpin them all.

Once you have your evidence for assessment, it needs to be judged. According to its definition, the act of 'judging' simply means forming an opinion or conclusion about something. In everyday use, the word 'judgement' has slightly negative connotations. That may be because it is most often used to describe the process of arriving at a negative opinion! In educational assessment, the judging of evidence is at least as likely to result in a positive opinion or conclusion, so the process of making that judgement should not be one for the student to fear or the teacher to avoid.

We all make judgements every day. The judgements we make might be about whether one thing is better or worse than another. For example, this bowl of soup might be delicious and that one much less so. On the other hand, some of the judgements we make are not intended to suggest that one thing is better than the other. For example, I might make the judgement that my friend is excited or bored, or this colour looks warmer than that one – without implying any criticism or approval.

Even as very young children, we make judgements – about food, about comfort, about who is familiar and safe and who might not be. More sophisticated judgements are added to our repertoire as we develop our capacities to make them. Many of the judgements we make result in decisions which might be to take action or not to do so (which is also a decision). Do I need to take an umbrella? Does this food stall look hygienic? Should my tone be more assertive? Is this path dangerous? Am I happy in this job? Should I get a dog? All of these assessments are important to the person making them, to varying degrees. We carry out assessments – make judgements – all the time, many of which have

Educational assessment and the role of the teacher

important consequences for us. In educational assessment, judgement is simply the process of forming an opinion or reaching a conclusion based upon evidence of learning. Once the judgement is made, decisions and actions can be taken!

> In educational assessment, judgement is the process of forming an opinion or reaching a conclusion based upon the evidence of learning presented.

Educational assessment: purpose and consequences, timing, frequency and formality

We have seen that traditional tests and exams have a very long history. We are so familiar with them that it is easy to assume that these are the 'normal' and 'best' approach to educational assessment and have a rigour that other kinds of assessment don't. In this book, we encourage you to think afresh about educational assessment, including this most traditional of approaches to it, because educational assessment comes in many shapes and sizes.

Assessment is happening every time a teacher deliberately scans a classroom to see who is engaged, who is working confidently, who looks bored, who looks puzzled or who is looking around for help or for distraction. Those actions may be fleeting – even somewhat unconscious – but they require a process of gathering evidence and making judgements, which is exactly what happens in all kinds of educational assessment.

Educational assessment is devised for different purposes. We will consider purpose in much more detail in Chapter 4, but for now, we can say that the consequences of any educational assessment follow from its purpose, and the timing, frequency and formality of assessment are related to those purposes and consequences.

Classroom Assessment for Teachers

> The timing, frequency and formality of any kind of assessment are usually related to its purpose and consequences.

We use the term 'formal' to mean something carried out in a carefully planned and executed way because the purpose and consequences of the assessment are especially important. We could apply that term to international assessments and to assessment for national qualifications, for example.

There are important relationships between the why, the when and the how of assessment. For example, according to its purpose (about which more, later) some educational assessment happens only occasionally and has important consequences and so would usually be quite formal in nature – it would be carefully planned and executed. Other kinds of educational assessment happen very frequently and can

Table 1.1 Purpose, consequences, timing, frequency and formality of educational assessment

Purpose	Consequences of each assessment	Timing	Frequency	Formality
To guide learning	Tends to be low	During learning	Continuous	Tends to be low
To check and record learning	Can be low to high	After learning	Occasional	Can be low to high
To identify learning difficulties or starting points for learning	Fairly high	As required	As required	Tends to be high

be very informal if the consequences of each assessment are much less significant.

Teachers have a role to play in all kinds of educational assessment but a lesser role in some than in others.

The role of the teacher in externally devised assessment

There are some formal assessments undertaken only occasionally in the academic year, with very significant consequences for students and for others. Because of those significant consequences, such assessments tend to be developed, tested and quality assured by experts and external organisations of various kinds. You may have some choice over which assessment to use and when, and you may be involved in administering some of these assessments, but in many cases, your role will simply be to prepare students for assessment or to make use of the outcomes of the assessment.

Assessments of this kind would include

- Routine assessments published by commercial organisations, intended as timesavers or support for teachers.
- Expert-devised assessment to diagnose particular learning difficulties such as dyslexia. In this case, the role of the teacher is to identify when such difficulties might be a barrier to learning, arrange for an appropriate test to be administered and act upon its outcomes.
- Assessment for national or state qualifications, in which many students might undertake an assessment at the same time. The teacher's role is primarily to prepare students for the assessment as well as possible.
- International assessments such as TIMSS (Trends in International Mathematics and Science Study) and PIRLS (Progress in International Reading Literacy Study), which are used by many countries to gauge how their education system is performing. In this case, the role of the teacher is to prepare students for assessment and sometimes to help administer it.

Classroom Assessment for Teachers

- Standardised national or state assessments that may be taken by all or a sample of students. (Where such assessments are digital, they might be automatically tailored to each student and taken when the student is ready.) In this case, the role of the teacher is to prepare students for assessment and usually to administer it.
- Fairly formal assessment given at the start of a period of learning to determine where a new student is in their learning and used to inform decisions about which courses of learning are suitable for a student.

These examples of educational assessment are usually developed, tested, distributed and marked or quality assured by others, and the role of the teacher is relatively limited. This book is not concerned with any of these externally produced assessments other than to note that the principles described in this book should apply to all educational assessments, including these.

If you have the opportunity to choose an assessment, then it will helpful for you to understand what good assessment looks like in order to make an appropriate choice. Even if you have little say over the choice of an assessment for your students, it will be valuable for you to understand its purpose and how it tries to achieve that, in order to prepare your students for it. You may also have an opportunity to contribute to an evaluation of such assessments, and an understanding of the underlying principles will help you to do that with relevant knowledge and appropriate confidence.

Teacher-devised classroom assessment

Teachers have a much greater role to play in most other kinds of classroom assessment. Teacher-devised educational assessment happens whenever the teacher is focused on students and judging evidence of their learning. Some kinds of educational assessment happen many times a day, almost continuously, involving judgements by the student or the teacher or both. We would describe these approaches to educational assessment as relatively unplanned and informal. The judging of evidence of learning is certainly occurring, but those judgements may not be formally recorded and that evidence of learning might not be formally collected. This kind of assessment, though, will still have important outcomes in the form of immediate feedback to students and the learning that results. It is always important to be thoughtful about the evidence you're looking for, to be confident that your judgements on that evidence are well founded, and to be careful about the ways in which you use those judgements to provide feedback to your students.

Examples of these kinds of relatively unplanned and informal assessment would include

- The teacher observing a student or a group of students and making assessment judgements on the basis of those observations
- The teacher interacting with students, looking together at work that is being or has been done, discussing that work and agreeing upon next steps
- The student being involved in identifying evidence for assessment, perhaps asking for feedback on work from the teacher or from another student or gathering work in a personal portfolio of some kind

All of these kinds of assessments can be somewhat informal (although observing students and personal portfolios can also be part of a much more formal assessment process). The outcomes of such assessment may or may not be recorded, but if the outcomes have consequences for students, then these assessments should still follow the principles that guide and underpin all good assessment. While all educational assessment should be guided by the same principles, when assessment is very frequent and the consequences of each one are relatively modest, a more dynamic, informal approach can be taken.

Classroom Assessment for Teachers

> When assessment is frequent and the consequences of each instance are quite low, then a more dynamic and informal approach to assessment is possible.

The kinds of educational assessment that teachers are most often involved in devising, and that will be the primary focus of this book, would include the following, which have different purposes and consequences, timing, frequency and formality:

- Assessment during a course of learning – and there may be many of these occasions – the primary purpose of which is to inform next steps in learning. The extent to which this kind of assessment is formalised will vary from teacher to teacher and from classroom to classroom.
- Assessment after a period of learning, to determine whether the anticipated knowledge and skills have been developed. This can happen when the teacher thinks an individual student is ready to be assessed or the whole class may take an assessment at the same time as a kind of 'checkpoint'. The outcomes of such assessment can be recorded and can also be used for reporting purposes, such as in an end-of-term report.

Relationships between these two kinds of assessment and the important factors of purpose, consequences, timing, frequency and formality are shown in Table 1.2.

Whatever the purpose, consequences, timing, frequency and formality of assessment, all good educational assessment should possess the important qualities that we introduce in **Chapter 2**, and should offer benefits to your students and minimise risks of harm to them, as we explain in **Chapter 3**. These represent the key principles that guide the creation of educational assessment in most systems across the world.

Educational assessment and the role of the teacher

Table 1.2 Consequences, timing, frequency and formality of assessment, according to purpose

Purpose	Consequences of each assessment	Timing	Frequency	Formality
To inform next steps in learning	Tends to be low if frequency is sufficiently high	During learning	Frequent	Tends to be low
To check whether the planned learning has occurred	Can be low to high, depending on how the teacher uses the assessment outcomes	At the end of a period of learning	Occasional, as required	Can be low to high, according to consequences

If you are devising educational assessment for your students in your classrooms, then you will likely have complete control over, and responsibility for, the quality of those assessments and the ways in which the outcomes of those assessments are used. Good assessment comes from having a defined purpose (**Chapter 4**), being clear about who you will assess (**Chapter 5**), knowing exactly what you want to assess and so what evidence you need to see (**Chapter 6**). You will then want to think carefully about how best to go about getting that evidence for assessment (**Chapter 7**), how to generate tasks for assessment if you need to (**Chapter 8**) and how best to judge any evidence that is either gathered or generated (**Chapter 9**). Finally, you will want to use the outcomes of assessment appropriately and with care (**Chapter 10**). We have translated the principles that underpin all good educational assessment into a number of practical steps that you can take to make sure your own assessment is good and is fit for your purposes.

Classroom Assessment for Teachers

Summary

In this chapter, we provided everyday contexts for the valuable activities of measuring, assessing and judging. We gave an overview of how educational assessment has developed from its beginnings, 1000 years ago, and continues to develop. Educational assessment should be coherent with approaches to curriculum and pedagogy, but, in all cases, we would define educational assessment as 'the judging of evidence of learning'. The conclusion of such judgement can be positive or negative. Evidence for assessment can be tangible or intangible, and it might occur naturally in the course of learning or be deliberately generated using an assessment task. Different kinds of educational assessment differ in their purpose, consequences, timing, frequency and formality. For some kinds of classroom assessment, the teacher's role is limited. For other kinds, the teacher will likely have control over, and responsibility for, the quality of those assessments. Those assessments are likely to have either formative or summative purposes. The chapters that follow describe the principles that underpin all good educational assessment and translate these into practical steps for devising good assessment, whatever its purpose.

2 The qualities of all good educational assessment
Validity, reliability, fairness and practicality

This chapter is all about

- The four qualities we look for in all educational assessment: validity, reliability, fairness and practicality
- How those qualities relate to and influence each other
- How to develop these qualities and how to avoid eroding them
- Balancing the qualities according to assessment purpose

Before we get on to the chapters that describe the practicalities of how to devise good assessment – assessment that is fit for purpose – it's important to understand the qualities that *all* good educational assessment should have. The decisions you will make when devising assessment will determine the extent to which it has these qualities.

There are four qualities that we look for in all good assessment – validity, reliability, fairness and practicality – and there are important relationships between them. In this chapter, we will see what these qualities are, how we create them, how they relate to each other and how to balance them in assessment that is fit for purpose. Most of these qualities are fundamental to good assessment, whether you are measuring length or weight, speed or strength, blood pressure or anxiety, knowledge of history or hairdressing skills. And all are fundamental in educational assessment, whatever the subject of that assessment might be.

> We look for validity, reliability, fairness and practicality in all good educational assessment.

Validity

For assessment to be valid, it should generate, and appropriately judge, evidence that is relevant and sufficient for us to know what a student knows and can do, or what it means when a student has passed or failed to pass, or been awarded grade A or grade C, grade B or grade D.

Validity is the extent to which an assessment measures what it means to measure. I use a tape rule to measure the width of a room because I want to be *sure* that big, new sofa is going to fit. If my blood pressure is taken, I need to be able to trust that the numbers it produces do indeed reveal what's important about my blood pressure so that my doctor and I can be confident about the steps we might each need to take to improve it. Both the tape rule and the blood pressure monitor measure exactly what they were intended to measure and so both have high levels of validity. Validity is the most important quality that any kind of assessment can have. If an assessment is valid, it will tell you what you need to know.

> If assessment is valid, it will tell you what you need to know.

The starting point for creating valid assessment is to be very clear about exactly what it is you want to know. If an assessment is valid, then it will measure only what it is intended to measure, and we can have confidence in what the outcomes of that assessment are telling

The qualities of all good educational assessment

us. That may be how much a student knows about our solar system or how well a student can apply knowledge of algebra, how skilful the student is at cake decoration or how much creativity the student can apply to a problem-solving task. Whatever is being measured, a valid assessment will provide information about *that thing* – information upon which everyone can depend.

On the other hand, assessment that lacks validity will produce outcomes that are unhelpful or misleading to some extent. Unhelpful because they aren't fit for our purpose if they don't help us confidently to identify what a student knows and can do, to the level of detail we require. Misleading because what that assessment is measuring is not quite what we intended although we may think that it is.

For example, it may be a maths test that requires a lot of reading or a reading test that needs some knowledge of horse racing. It may be an assessment of history that requires a lot of writing, or a writing assessment that assumes some knowledge of history. If an assessment of creativity rewards tidy work, then it is not only creativity that is being measured. If an assessment of knowledge requires students to make a presentation, then introverts may be disadvantaged. In each case, the outcomes of the assessment will be affected by something other than its intended focus, which will reduce the validity of that assessment. A valid assessment will be focused only on what is important for that assessment: its outcomes will not be influenced by irrelevant knowledge, skills, attributes or other characteristics.

Validity and assessment purpose

One way to think about validity is that it is a kind of 'fitness for purpose'. For example, a wooden or rigid plastic ruler with accurate markings is a valid instrument for the measurement of length, provided it is used with care. A piece of string could be a perfectly valid instrument for comparing lengths if your purpose is to know whether your piece of furniture will fit into a new location. It would not be a good enough instrument to use for making that piece of furniture, or for carpeting the room or building the house! The laser measure, the ruler and the piece of string are all valid instruments for measuring length, but each offers different amounts of information. Each can tell us what we need to know provided we have chosen the right one for the job. So, when thinking about the validity of an assessment, we should always be thinking about validity for a particular purpose. An assessment should always be created to be valid for a particular purpose.

> Assessment should be valid for a particular purpose.

Devising valid assessment

Ensuring validity should be the top priority throughout the process of devising assessment and the first thing we look for when evaluating one. Validity is created and maintained by all of the decisions we make throughout the process of assessment, from initial ideas about purpose and focus to how the outcomes of assessment are ultimately used. Validity is very easily lost at any point, from the very beginning to the very end of the process of assessment. For that reason, validity should always be at the forefront of your mind when devising or evaluating assessment.

> Validity is established as assessment is devised, and it can be easily lost at any point during that process or as assessment is carried out.

The qualities of all good educational assessment

Reliability

When we use the word 'reliable' in everyday life, we tend to mean something that is dependable. We like our cars to be reliable – and our friends. We depend on them and hope not to be let down by them.

In assessment, reliability has a slightly different meaning from the everyday one. The reliability of assessment can be thought of as a kind of 'signal to noise ratio'. The 'signal' comes from the important information that you're really looking for because it contributes usefully to the assessment of what you're interested in. The 'noise' comes from anything else that messes up or obscures that signal to some extent. The higher the signal and the lower the noise, the better the reliability of the assessment.

Let's think about a very simple example of this. Imagine that you want to assess how quickly students can walk a 1-mile distance. The important 'signal' information is the time taken for each student to complete the walk – between starting and finishing. Let's suppose that the students clearly understand the assessment requirements: that they need to walk the distance as quickly as possible. Unless you specify clearly what surface they walk along, 'noise' could result from some students walking for 1 mile along a flat road and others walking for 1 mile up a hill, or some taking the assessment on a hot day and others on a windy one. It could come from students wearing different kinds of footwear. It could result from all assessors not recording start and finish times carefully and accurately. Another kind of 'noise' could result because the assessment disadvantages a whole group of students with particular walking difficulties, for example. Even more 'noise' would be introduced if the assessment task isn't clear to students, and some of them stop to enjoy the view and others run all the way! You can see that there are many ways in which even a simple assessment like this could become very unreliable unless the task is clear, the conditions under which it is taken are the same for everyone, all students have access to the necessary resources and the assessors do a consistent and good job. We will talk about all of these things later in the book.

Classroom Assessment for Teachers

In theory, an assessment is reliable if it would give the same outcome when used to assess the same thing or person on different occasions. For many kinds of assessment or measurement, it is possible to test and evaluate this kind of reliability. For example, we can test the reliability of a new design of ruler by using it to carefully measure and record the length of something many times in the conditions in which it is intended to be used. If we get the same measured length each time, then we know it is a reliable instrument.

Of course, measuring learning is not as simple as measuring length. To test educational assessment for the kind of reliability we expect a ruler to have, we would need to be able to measure a student in exactly the same way on at least two occasions. The assessment would need to be the same and the student would need to be, too; for example, they would need to have the same amount of energy, preparation and learning on those two assessment occasions. The conditions under which the assessment is undertaken would need to be the same: same temperature, same background noise, same time of day. Importantly, the student would need to have absolutely no recollection of the first assessment! And, of course, the judging of that evidence for assessment would need to be done in exactly the same way each time.

We can't test for this kind of reliability in this way (we do have other ways, though), but that thinking helps us to understand the kinds of things that can make assessment unreliable. Many of those things we can't control, but for reliable assessment, we should control all we can. Specifying the conditions under which an assessment is taken can make an important contribution to assessment reliability. One common cause of unreliability in educational assessment is unclear instructions to the student or to the assessor. And bias towards or against particular groups of students is also a big risk to reliability. We will say more about all of these things in later chapters.

Where there is repeated assessment in the classroom, assessment reliability may be less important if the consequences of each assessment are low. If a student performs well on most assessments, then the occasional

The qualities of all good educational assessment

poor performance becomes less significant. It is in this way that repeating assessment can improve its reliability. That's the reason that carpenters quickly learn to measure more than once before cutting the wood!

The relationship between reliability and validity

Imagine a ruler – Ruler 1 – made of a material that expands when warm and contracts when cold. This would not be a reliable instrument if it was to be used in an environment where the temperature fluctuates. The instrument would expand on a hot day and so the measured width of a shelf on that day would be less than its measured width on a cold day. That measurement would be affected by factors unrelated to the shelf's actual width, caused by an unreliable instrument, which is, therefore, also not a valid one. Reliability makes an important contribution to validity.

Now imagine Ruler 2, made of relatively stable and inert material such as wood and with accurate markings. Used with care, this instrument will give the same measured shelf width every time, regardless of how hot the day might be. That measured width of the shelf will be accurate and so this instrument is both valid and reliable.

Finally, imagine Ruler 3, made of wood but the markings on this ruler are incorrect. This ruler would give exactly the same width each time the shelf is measured, but that measured width would be incorrect! Ruler 3 would be reliable since it would give exactly the same – incorrect – measured width each time it was used. But it would not be valid since the measured width would be meaningless. Reliability is important for validity, but it is not sufficient: a reliable assessment is not always a valid one.

Reliability and assessment purpose

In educational assessment, some see reliability and validity as always in tension. As we saw with Ruler 1, assessment cannot be valid if it is not sufficiently reliable. Reliability contributes to validity in a very important way. On the other hand, good assessment should not maximise reliability at the cost of validity. Assessment devised primarily for summative purposes is often particularly concerned with reliability. When summative assessment might have significant consequences for students – determining opportunities for further learning or employment, for example – it is natural and reasonable to expect it to be highly reliable. But there is always a risk that efforts to maximise reliability can reduce assessment validity. For example, you might be tempted to increase reliability of an assessment of practical science skills by testing knowledge of science equipment in a written test. That would certainly be easier to mark reliably, and it would be a valid assessment of such knowledge, but it would probably not be a valid assessment of practical science skills.

Without validity, the assessment cannot tell us what we need to know, no matter how reliable it is. It is vitally important to maintain validity and, at the same time, to try to make assessment as reliable as possible, and there are many ways to do that as we will see in later chapters.

Fairness

Fairness is seldom an issue when measuring length, but it is hugely important in educational assessment. There is an everyday understanding of 'fairness', and its meaning in assessment is similar in many ways. If there is one quality of assessment that everyone feels they understand, *and understand its importance,* it is fairness. The feeling of being the victim of unfairness is acutely painful, as most 5-year-olds know. But what exactly is fairness when we're talking about educational assessment?

Fairness in educational assessment

There are different ways to think about fairness in educational assessment. The most obvious one is that assessment should not discriminate against particular groups. A fair assessment should reward students

The qualities of all good educational assessment

or discriminate between them only on the basis of relevant evidence, not on irrelevant characteristics or factors such as gender or socio-economic group.

> A fair assessment should reward or penalise students only on the basis of what is relevant to the assessment.

In another sense, you might feel an assessment is fair if its outcomes reflect the work you did to prepare for it. Conversely, it would feel unfair if it was much too hard for everyone, as sometimes happens in assessment for national qualifications. In that case, the marks required for each grade can be adjusted, but the stress felt during such an assessment can, itself, affect assessment outcomes negatively and to a different extent for different students.

It might be considered fair to apply the same rules to everyone – by assessment markers, for example. On the other hand, some would argue that it might be fairer to treat students differently if they have bigger hurdles to jump. In some important assessments, students with dyslexia are given more time to complete the assessment. Is that fair?

And there is also a sense in which fairness is about meeting everyone's expectations – there being no nasty surprises in assessment.

Relationships between fairness, reliability and validity

Assessment professionals debate the relative importance of different kinds of fairness in educational assessment, but all can have an important impact. And there are important interactions among fairness, validity and reliability.

Classroom Assessment for Teachers

A fair assessment is one that

- Allows all students, as far as possible, to show what they know and can do (for fairness and validity)
- Is undertaken in equitable conditions by all students (for fairness, reliability and validity)
- Is judged impartially and in line with clear instructions (for fairness, reliability and validity)

By contrast, an unfair assessment is one in which some students do not have the expected opportunity to do well, for one reason or another, or for a number of reasons. For example, an assessment that is not of reading skills but that requires a lot of reading may unnecessarily disadvantage students with dyslexia or those for whom the assessment is not in their first language. Assessment might use a context that is unfamiliar to some students or might assume background knowledge that not all students have. If instructions for judging evidence for assessment are not clear, the outcomes may be influenced by bias on the part of assessors. An assessment that requires a lot of time outside of the classroom to prepare for or to undertake may not be fair to those with caring responsibilities or other significant demands on their time or to those without quiet space or the necessary resources at home.

Assessment should ensure that no groups of students are disadvantaged. If you are devising assessment for your own students, you will likely know them well and be in a very good position to ensure that your assessment is fair to them all. An unfair assessment cannot be valid or reliable, as it will not allow every student an equitable opportunity show what they know and can do. Fairness in educational assessment is ethical, and it also impacts in important ways upon assessment validity and reliability.

The qualities of all good educational assessment

> Ethical assessment should be fair, and fairness also impacts upon other qualities of good educational assessment.

Fair assessment is good for everyone

Fairness should be built into assessment from the start. That will be helped by having a very clear focus on what it is *essential* to assess. It may be that some assessments *must* exclude some students, by the nature of what is to be assessed. For example, assessment of dance, athletics or bricklaying may quite reasonably be inaccessible to someone with severe physical limitations. Some music or aural assessments may reasonably be inaccessible to someone who is profoundly deaf. Fairness doesn't mean that every assessment should be able to be undertaken in the same way by every student: it is about making sure that an assessment does not *unnecessarily* disadvantage any individuals or groups.

Special arrangements can increase the accessibility of many assessments. Organisations with responsibility for awarding qualifications may call these 'access arrangements' or 'reasonable adjustments', and there is a careful process for determining such arrangements. They are intended to make sure that students can undertake the assessment despite having special educational needs, disabilities or temporary needs that might reduce their access to an assessment. Such arrangements might include additional time, readers, scribes or other support designed to meet the needs of the individual student. These should remove irrelevant barriers without reducing the intended challenge of the assessment.

Classroom Assessment for Teachers

But all assessments should be created to be as accessible as possible without any special arrangements having to be made. If the intended focus of the assessment does not reasonably exclude certain groups, then every effort should be made – from the start – to ensure that all students can access that assessment and have an equitable opportunity to do well in it. Such an approach should benefit all students.

> Assessment that is carefully devised to be inclusive and fair to all students will be better assessment for everyone.

Many assessment professionals are interested in the concept of inclusive assessment and the practical means of achieving it. Inclusive assessment focusses on how assessment can proactively minimise the chances of students being excluded or disadvantaged by the ways in which they are assessed. Inclusive assessments usually aim for a balance of tasks, undertaken under different conditions (more on this later) and at different times across a course of learning. Inclusive assessment was initially focused on ensuring that students with particular needs were not excluded or disadvantaged by assessment, but it is now recognised as good practice that benefits *all* students being assessed.

Practicality

Practicality is last on the list but almost as important as the other three qualities because it can have important impacts on all of them. Just like validity, reliability and fairness, practicality should be kept carefully in mind from the beginning of the process of devising assessment and throughout that process. No matter how much thought goes into ensuring an assessment's validity, reliability and fairness, if it is not sufficiently practical, then all three of those important qualities

The qualities of all good educational assessment

will likely be compromised. Ideally, an assessment should not require unreasonable resources, including time, and it should not need unreasonable assessor training. Also, a good measure of practicality is that students don't need a lot of 'exam practice' to understand clearly what they need to do in the assessment in order to do well.

Of course, practicality is always something to be aspired to. Generally speaking, nobody wants to spend two days cooking one perfect meal; nobody wants to buy a vacuum cleaner that you need a degree in engineering to operate; and there is very little demand for hand-held lawnmowers. So practicality is always a sensible thing to strive for.

Practicality just makes sense, but in educational assessment, there are other important reasons to strive for it. Topping any other reason for ensuring your educational assessment is practical to use is the risk that any lack of practicality will undermine your assessment's validity, reliability and fairness.

Relationships between practicality and fairness, reliability and validity

If students and classrooms don't *all* have ready access to necessary resources, or if assessors need a lot of training, or if students can only do well if they have lots of coaching on 'exam technique', that assessment will not be highly valid, reliable or fair. The fairness and also the validity of assessment will be reduced if it can't be carried out as intended because not all students have the same time or resources they need to prepare for or undertake the assessment. The fairness and reliability, and so also the validity, of an assessment will be reduced if not all students receive the same coaching in 'exam technique' or have the same access to the 'secret knowledge' about an assessment that only exam markers might have. The reliability, and so also the validity, of an assessment will be reduced if only some markers have the specialist training or the time they need to mark according to complex instructions. These are just some practical considerations. You could create an assessment that could be the most valid, reliable and fair

Classroom Assessment for Teachers

assessment in the world, but if it's not practical, it won't be done as you intended and so all of that validity, reliability and fairness will be undermined.

> Any lack of practicality will undermine assessment's validity, reliability and fairness.

Practicality and assessment purpose

It is always important to consider the purpose of assessment. Assessment of the competence of an aspiring brain surgeon or super-tanker deck officer may well justify lengthy or complex assessment with highly specialised resources. It may need highly trained teachers and assessors, and students may need a lot of assessment preparation. The same would be true of other professions with life-and-death consequences. In such situations, the most important thing is that assessment is highly valid, reliable and fair, even if it means that practicality is lower down the list of priorities. But most other assessments would not justify similarly time-consuming and resource-intensive preparation and assessment. Like validity and reliability, practicality should always be considered in relation to the purpose of the assessment. Sometimes, it is reasonable that an assessment requires a lot of time or resources to undertake; more often, it is not. Good assessment should be as practicable as possible for its intended purpose without compromising its validity, reliability and fairness.

> Assessment should be as practical as possible for its purpose.

The qualities of all good educational assessment

Getting the balance right for assessment that is fit for purpose

The qualities of validity, reliability, fairness and practicality are applicable to all educational assessment, to a greater or lesser extent according to assessment purpose. But the qualities of good assessment are not all-or-nothing. Educational assessment should aim to be highly valid, reliable, fair and practicable, but none is completely so and we have seen that there are usually balances to be struck. Despite our best efforts, no perfect educational assessment has yet been created. However, creating good assessment – assessment that is fit for purpose – requires us to try to optimise these critical qualities of validity, reliability, fairness and practicality.

> The qualities of all good assessment should be balanced according to purpose.

Summary

In this chapter, we introduced the four qualities that all educational assessment should have: validity, reliability, fairness and practicality. We explained what each of these is and why it is important. Validity is the extent to which an assessment is measuring what it says it will. Reliability is the extent to which assessment is free from the impacts of irrelevant factors, and we gave examples of different kinds of risks to assessment reliability. Assessment fairness can be viewed in different ways but is fundamentally the extent to which all students, as far as possible, can show what they know and can do. Practicality is the extent to which assessment is manageable for both student and assessor. We described ways in which these qualities interact with each another and showed how reliability, fairness and practicality

Classroom Assessment for Teachers

all contribute to the validity of an assessment. We also explained the ways in which these qualities can be undermined by poor decisions when assessment is being devised and why the extent to which validity, reliability, and practicality are each required of an assessment relates to its purpose.

3 The ethics of educational assessment

This chapter is all about

- The benefits of educational assessment
- Potential risks associated with educational assessment
- Why we need to consider the ethics of educational assessment

In Chapter 1, we explored what educational assessment *is*, with timing, frequency and formality determined by assessment purpose and consequences. Every educational assessment has consequences. Even a passing comment on a piece of work can have an impact on a student's confidence and sense of competence as a learner and on the relationship between student and teacher. The impacts of the kinds of educational assessment in which the outcomes are recorded or the evidence retained can be even more significant.

Educational assessment can range from very infrequent and formal to very frequent and relatively informal, but all educational assessment has the potential to have both positive and negative impacts upon the student. There can be immediate impacts on a student's learning and also on their self-esteem and engagement in education or in society, as well as on their long-term life chances. Those important consequences must be a primary consideration for anyone devising or using educational assessment.

Classroom Assessment for Teachers

> All educational assessment has the potential for both positive and negative impacts upon students and others.

What kinds of good can educational assessment do?

When assessment is well-devised, it can have positive impacts on students and their learning. For example, such assessment can

- Provide students with opportunities to show what they know and can do
- Increase student understanding and enthusiasm for learning
- Provide important information to the teacher and the student to inform and guide future learning
- Keep both student and teacher focused on what is important
- Offer an enjoyable challenge for students

If you have been lucky enough to experience good assessment, you will remember feeling the sense of achievement that can come with it or the motivation that comes with understanding what assessment outcomes mean. You may have felt proud and pleased to show what you had learned, or you may have viewed your assessment outcome as an opportunity to correct your misunderstandings and learn more. Your assessment may have reminded you about what's important in a topic that you learned some time ago, or you may have just enjoyed the fun of classroom quizzes! Educational assessment can provide students with important opportunities to show what they know and can do, to motivate and reward.

> One of the important benefits of educational assessment is that it can provide students with opportunities to show what they know and can do which can motivate and reward their efforts.

The ethics of educational assessment

What kinds of harm can educational assessment do?

Conversely, poorly devised assessment can have negative impacts on students and their learning. For example, such assessment can

- Confuse or mislead students about their own abilities
- De-motivate students by damaging their self-confidence or causing them to feel unfairly treated
- Misinform student and teacher about progression in learning and confuse students about what's important in their learning
- Cause unhelpful stress

Poorly devised educational assessment can harm students' wellbeing and progression in learning. Since you are reading this book it's likely that you have usually done quite well in educational assessments. Can you imagine how it would feel to more often have 'failed' in some way and how that would make you feel about education and about yourself?

You may remember being assessed at some time in the past in a way that caused you harm or you felt at the time as though it had. That stressful exam that caused you to freeze so you couldn't complete it. The embarrassment of a very low score on a physics test that put you off the subject. Those little tests you did well in but that didn't prepare you for the final assessment in which you were shocked to do badly. The questions in an agriculture exam on which those students who grew up on an organic farm did better because of personal knowledge. All those assessments when you ran out of time to show what you knew and could do! Experiences like this can disrupt progression in learning, in both short and longer terms.

> We also need to beware of the risks that educational assessment can pose to learning and to learner wellbeing.

Classroom Assessment for Teachers

Beyond its potential impacts on student learning and wellbeing, educational assessment offers risks and benefits to wider society, too. We depend on the outcomes of assessment to make the right choices of career for ourselves. Employers, colleges and universities need to be able to use the outcomes of assessment to make good choices in their recruitment. Assessment of train drivers, engineers, doctors and pilots can have life-or-death consequences! Getting assessment right is important for everyone.

The ethics of educational assessment

In many societies, assessment has been part of education for a very long time. As a result, we may tend to accept that it is a good and necessary thing. We don't question that assumption, and we don't examine closely the ways in which we *do* assessment. Assessment professionals are increasingly questioning why and how we carry out educational assessment so that they can help us to maximise its positive effects and minimise its negative effects. Just because assessment has been part of education for as long as we can remember, we shouldn't think that we cannot question its practices and assumptions. For example, tests and exams have come in for a lot of criticism in recent years. If tests and exams are devised to discriminate between students, then you might conclude they are expected to create 'failures', and many would question the morality of that.

In medicine, we are familiar with the principle of 'first, do no harm'. In fact, in medical ethics, the aim is to do as much good as possible while minimising any harms. The first step in trying to maximise the benefits and minimise the harms of educational assessment is to ensure that assessment is of good quality. That it is valid, reliable, practical and fair. That it is fit for purpose. In addition, for ethical reasons and also because it contributes to assessment validity, the student needs to know when assessment could or will happen. They should also be informed about, and might even be included in decisions about, what forms assessment will take, how evidence for assessment will be

The ethics of educational assessment

judged and what use will be made of the outcomes of that assessment. Whether it happens at the end of the year in an exam hall or many times a day in the classroom, students should be confident that they know what they need to do in order to do well in any assessment.

There are other ethical issues around assessment. Assessment that disadvantages or excludes an individual or group is clearly unethical as is one that is biased in favour of a particular group. Bad assessment can be unfair to individuals or groups; it can damage trust in teachers and the system; it may waste the time of students and teachers; and it could mislead those who make use of assessment outcomes.

Don't be disheartened! We tend to remember occasional harms done to us more readily than we do all those occasions when things went well. It is on those occasions that educational assessment has had its positive impacts: giving us a chance to show (and show off!) what we know and can do; helping our teachers to understand us better and better support our future learning; engaging and challenging us in an enjoyable way; or furnishing us with qualifications that opened doors to future learning and to work. Take a moment to remember the assessment that felt absolutely right, for which you felt ready and in which you did well. Remember those great assessment outcomes that felt like a just reward for all your hard work and gave you confidence that you were on the right learning path. And those disappointing ones that, nevertheless, felt fair, that helped you to change direction without regrets. If an assessment is valid, reliable, fair and practical, you can much more readily accept a disappointing outcome and use it with confidence to make decisions about the future.

> If an assessment is valid, reliable, fair and practical, you can use its outcome with more confidence.

Classroom Assessment for Teachers

There is currently no widely accepted, formal framework for ethical assessment in education. Until there is, the key thing to remember is that educational assessment offers many benefits to students as well as to society, but the risks can be great, too. The ethics of educational assessment require us to maximise its benefits and minimise its risks, and the principles that underpin all good educational assessment help us to do just that.

> The ethics of educational assessment require us to maximise its benefits and minimise its risks.

Summary

In this chapter, we described the benefits and risks of educational assessment. While well-devised assessment can boost student motivation, guide future learning and enhance understanding, poorly devised assessments can harm students by causing confusion, de-motivation and stress. Ethical issues arise when assessments are unfair, biased or disadvantage certain individuals or groups. For ethical assessment, you should inform your students about any assessment and how you will use its outcomes. Despite the potential harms, if you devise your assessment well, it can significantly benefit students by providing them with opportunities to demonstrate their knowledge and skills and to learn from the outcomes of assessment. On the other hand, poorly devised assessment can disrupt your students' progress and cause other harms. We stress the need to maximise benefits and minimise risks by devising ethical assessment that is valid, reliable, fair and practical.

Section 2
Practical steps for devising good assessment in the classroom

4 Be clear about why you want to assess

This chapter is all about

- The importance of having a clear purpose for assessment: for ethical reasons and for assessment validity
- Common purposes for classroom assessment: formative, summative and diagnostic

Because of the potential harms of educational assessment, we should never do it without a good reason! Not only that, good assessment should be devised with a particular purpose in mind that informs all of the decisions we make when devising assessment.

The purpose of assessment is all about the use you intend to make of the outcomes of that assessment. Will you use assessment outcomes to inform and help your students make progress in their learning? Will you use assessment outcomes to record a student's attainment for your own summary records or for reporting to parents? Will you use assessment outcomes to identify students with particular learning difficulties? Will you use it to identify students with a particular level of proficiency in order to allocate them to a particular class or group? As you think about how to devise your assessment – or to choose it (as in the case of most diagnostic assessment) – the first and most important question to ask yourself is: *why* do you want to assess?

> The first and most important question to ask when devising assessment is: *why* do you want to assess?

Assessment purpose informs everything

The key to devising good assessment is alignment. There should be a clear line of thought from assessment purpose through every decision about gathering or generating evidence for assessment, judging that evidence, and using assesment outcomes according to that purpose.

Every assessment is intended to tell us something important about what a student knows and can do, and exactly what is important depends on the purpose of our assessment. We might want to know how much a student already knows and can do, how much a student has learned, what a student hasn't understood or why a student is experiencing particular difficulties. Assessments are devised differently according to what we want to find out and the best assessment is therefore devised with a particular purpose in mind. Assessment purpose, and the related consequences of assessment, will determine things like timing, frequency and formality of assessment. It will inform every decision we make about what kinds of evidence for assessment are needed and how much, how best to obtain that evidence, how it should be judged, and how the resulting assessment outcomes could and shouldn't be used.

> Good assessment begins with purpose in mind.

Be clear about why you want to assess

Purposes of classroom assessment

We can usefully think about three main purposes for classroom assessment – formative, summative and diagnostic. The first two are purposes for which teacher-devised assessment is commonly used. In both formative and summative assessment, the outcomes of assessment can be used to determine what has been learned and how well. Where this information is used to guide future learning, the assessment has a formative purpose. Where it is used to record past learning, the assessment has a summative purpose.

It is common to talk of formative and summative assessment as though these are completely different things. In reality, to some extent the outcomes of any assessment can be used for either summative or formative purposes. For example, the grades recorded for an end of topic assessment might be accompanied by feedback that is shared with students and informs next steps in teaching and learning. In reporting to parents, you might include not only the outcomes of summative assessments but also the outcomes of some formative assessment that reveal what the student needs to do next to progress.

That said, it's normally easier to devise really good assessment with purpose in mind. Assessment devised for one purpose might also be able to be used for another purpose to some extent but likely won't work quite so well for that other purpose.

> Assessment devised with a purpose in mind will usually work better for that purpose than one that is not.

For example, an assessment intended for summative purposes might be more formal than one intended for formative purposes. The kinds of evidence for assessment that each should provide will likely be different. The ways in which that evidence should be judged might be different, and the outcomes each produces will almost certainly be different.

Assessment for summative purposes is used to determine the extent to which students have learned what was intended, and to some extent (in the case of assessment for national or professional qualifications, for example) might be devised to reveal differences between students. Assessment for formative purposes is used to reveal details of what has and has not been learned by an individual student. In each case, what you want to know and how you will use that information should determine how you will obtain the right kinds of evidence for assessment, how you will judge it, what form your assessment outcomes will take and how those outcomes can be used. The clearer the purpose of an assessment, the more fit for that purpose it can be. Assessment is best devised with purpose clearly in mind.

The third common purpose for classroom assessment is diagnostic. While some diagnostic assessment may be teacher-devised, much of it will have been developed and tested by others. We will touch on diagnostic assessment later in the chapter, but most of this chapter and this book is concerned with the assessment purposes for which the teacher is likely to have most responsibility – classroom assessment for formative (often called assessment *for* learning) and summative (often called assessment *of* learning) purposes.

Assessment for learning

As a teacher, your primary concern will be that your students make progress in their learning. You will want to understand where they are in their learning so that you can most effectively support them. This is the purpose of formative assessment, or 'assessment *for* learning'. Formative assessment tends to be fairly informal and quite frequent so that each assessment has only moderate consequences for students. That said, more formal assessment can also be readily used for

Be clear about why you want to assess

a formative purpose when it happens during learning and is devised for that purpose.

The purpose of formative assessment is to inform what teachers do and to help students to learn more effectively. Good formative assessment should help teacher and student to adjust their teaching and learning approaches to ensure that progress in learning continues to be made. There is evidence that formative assessment not only improves students' academic performance, but it also helps them to become better independent learners.

> Assessment with a formative purpose helps teacher and student to adjust their teaching and their learning.

Assessment for formative purposes might happen once a week, once a month, or many times daily, when an individual student's progress can be monitored and any misunderstandings addressed at an early stage and when the student can be most fully engaged in their own learning journey. Formative assessment is most likely to focus on the details of a student's work in order to produce the kinds of information you need for formative purposes. You will want evidence for what students know and can do but will also want to know where there are gaps in their knowledge or skills. To devise this kind of assessment, you need to know what it is you want your students to learn but also how learning tends to happen in that subject. What knowledge and skills would normally precede others, and what forms of activity would help students to build the knowledge and skills they need?

Since the purpose of such assessment is to identify and support the student's next steps in learning, the outcomes of it are used to provide feedback (some favour the term 'feed-forward') to students, to help

Classroom Assessment for Teachers

the student to progress and the teacher to facilitate that progression. Feedback can be immediate and narrowly focused, such as the identification of strengths in a piece of work and opportunities for improvement. It can also be used to work with the student to set relevant and achievable learning goals.

> Assessment for formative purposes will be most useful if it focusses on the details of a student's work, to inform adjustments in teaching and learning.

Students can focus on a grade or mark at the expense of any more constructive comment, so the outcomes of formative assessment would normally take the form of verbal or written advice for the student: qualitative feedback rather than marks or grades. Formative assessment can be most effective when lots of small, frequent assessments are used and when feedback is immediate. We revisit this later in the book.

KEY FEATURES OF ASSESSMENT DEVISED TO BE USED FOR FORMATIVE PURPOSES

Assessment that is intended to be used for formative purposes ('assessment for learning')

- Occurs during learning, quite frequently, and is usually informal in character
- Provides information that can be shared with the student on what they know and can do and what requires more attention
- Provides outcomes that will help the teacher and/or student to adjust their approaches to teaching and learning

Be clear about why you want to assess

Assessment of learning

Assessment that is devised for summative purposes should, first and foremost, be able to summarise the student's learning and achievements to date. The purpose of summative assessment is to find out what the student knows and can do at the end of a period of learning. That period might be short or long – anything from a short test at the end of a topic to assessment for national qualifications at the end of an extended period of learning.

> Assessment with a summative purpose provides a snapshot of what students know and can do at the end of a period of learning.

If you are devising assessment for summative purposes in your classroom, you will want it to tell you how much of the intended learning has, indeed, happened. You will want your assessment to provide and judge evidence for all of that intended learning or for an appropriate sample of it from which you can infer other knowledge and skills. Assessment for this purpose is sometimes known as 'assessment *of* learning'. Such assessment may be undertaken relatively occasionally and has consequences that can be quite important for students, so it might be fairly formal in character. You will want to know what students know and can do at the end of a period of learning by comparison with what you intended them to know and be able to do by that time.

> Assessment for summative purposes will be most useful if it provides information about how much of the expected knowledge and skills a student can demonstrate.

Classroom Assessment for Teachers

The outcomes of your summative assessment might be used for your own recording purposes or to report to students, parents and carers or to other members of staff. Such a report might be used to provide important information when a student moves to a new grade, to another school or learning institution, or from junior to senior schooling, for example.

Because the main purpose of summative assessment is often to report to those who may not be (and don't need to be) familiar with the details of a course of learning, the outcomes are usually very high level. For example, the assessment outcome might be reported as a simple 'pass' if certain criteria are met, as a single grade or sometimes a few grades or marks representing different levels of performance. In each case, it is intended to convey meaning to its users even without detailed knowledge of the course or period of learning being assessed. They may only understand that an 'A' grade in a particular subject is better than a 'B' grade, and a 'B' grade is better than a 'C' grade, and so on. This approach can be applied to internal assessment devised for summative purposes as well as to the kinds of externally set, marked or moderated assessment that is often associated with national qualifications and with national and international standardised assessments.

> The outcomes of summative assessment are intended to be meaningful to those without detailed knowledge of the learning being assessed.

Assessment with a primarily summative purpose with very significant consequences is perhaps most commonly used at the end of the student's school career. At this important transition, many students are expected to engage in high-stakes assessment (one for which the

Be clear about why you want to assess

consequences, or 'stakes', are high). Such assessment is often created, marked and/or moderated by an external organisation and the outcomes of the assessment used as the basis of some kind of school leaving certificate. The outcomes of summative assessment for national or professional qualifications are often used by those selecting students for further or higher education or for employment. This kind of summative assessment, therefore, has very important consequences for the student, as its outcomes can have a significant impact on future access to learning and to work.

Any summative assessment you devise for your own students will not likely have such significant consequences. There may be occasions when you want to devise summative assessment for your students to use the outcomes to provide a report for parents or carers. You may need to report how your students are doing to your department, faculty or school. You may want some kind of summary overview of student progress (such as in the form of a grade for each subject) for your own records and planning. For all of these reasons, you may decide that you need to devise assessment for summative purposes at the end of a course, term, unit or topic of learning. Or you may need to use, or have the opportunity to choose, an assessment created by others for this purpose. In the former case, you will want to devise assessment that is fit for your purposes. In the latter case, it will be useful to know what you're looking for in such assessment.

We have described a number of sensible uses of summative assessment, but before you decide to devise summative assessment for use in your own classroom, ask yourself these questions:

- Do you really need a summary of what has been learned at this point?
- Will you or someone else actually use the outcomes of such assessment?

If no one is going to use the outcomes of summative assessment, then it has no purpose and your time might be better spent on other things.

Classroom Assessment for Teachers

If you do decide to devise assessment for summative purposes, it should be intended to generate evidence of learning across the breadth and depth of expected learning. Such assessment is not primarily intended to identify gaps in learning. It is looking for evidence that the intended knowledge and skills have been gained rather than of specific areas of knowledge and skills that have not.

> Assessment for summative purposes should provide evidence for assessment across the breadth and depth of learning expected.

It is a common mistake to confuse lots of small summative assessments with formative assessment, for example to think that administering a lot of end-of-topic summative assessments, and giving back the outcomes of assessment, is a formative use of assessment. In reality, if assessment is designed to provide the kinds of evidence needed for summative purposes, it is unlikely to provide the kinds of evidence needed for formative ones. On top of that, if the outcomes of assessment include marks or grades, it is those that tend to matter most to the student. Even if some more formative feedback is also provided, students often focus mainly on their grade or mark and may not pay sufficient attention to the sorts of feedback that would really help them to progress in their learning. So, even if you try to use summative assessments for formative purposes, they may not work well because they have not been created with that purpose in mind. They are unlikely to provide the kinds of information you need to really help your students move forward in their learning.

Be clear about why you want to assess

> **KEY FEATURES OF ASSESSMENT DEVISED TO BE USED FOR SUMMATIVE PURPOSES**
>
> Assessment that is intended to be used for summative purposes ('assessment of learning')
>
> - Summarises what the student has achieved
> - Usually happens at the end of a course or period of learning and can be relatively formal in character
> - Produces outcomes that are a shorthand report for people who have not been involved in a course of learning, such as grades or marks
> - Is unlikely to be very effective for formative purposes

In the chapters that follow, we go into more detail about how to devise good assessment with purpose clearly in mind and about how the outcomes of assessment for formative and summative purposes can best be used.

Diagnostic assessment

The third common purpose for classroom assessment is diagnostic, commonly used before learning to inform decisions about appropriate course placement and during learning to identify the cause of particular difficulties a student may be having. Valid and reliable diagnostic assessment that is devised to confidently identify specific learning difficulties will normally have been created by experts who want to be able to compare student responses with those expected in an age-matched reference population. For example, assessments for dyslexia are important tools to ensure that a student with this specific learning difficulty gets diagnosed correctly and so gets the support they need to learn effectively. This kind of assessment is usually developed, tested and published by those with the necessary expertise, resources and access to data. The teacher's role is usually limited to recognising when such assessment is required, perhaps choosing a suitable assessment, administering it, and making appropriate use of the outcomes.

> Assessment for diagnostic purposes is usually based on making comparisons between student responses and those expected in the wider population and validated for that purpose.

To conclude, it is important to have a good reason for assessing your students and a clear idea of the primary purpose for your assessment. This will affect when you assess, how you assess and how you present and use the outcomes of the assessment. Whilst some assessments can be used for a variety of purposes, you are much more likely to succeed in your aims if you use an assessment that has been carefully created for the purpose you have in mind.

> **Practical Step 1:**
> *Always begin the process of devising assessment by being clear about why you want to assess your students, and keep that purpose in mind.*

Summary

In this chapter, we argued that any assessment should only be considered when it has a clear purpose. That's important for ethical reasons but also because assessment designed for a particular purpose is more

Be clear about why you want to assess

likely to be fit for that purpose. We outlined three common purposes for classroom assessment: formative, summative and diagnostic. These relate to the uses to which assessment outcomes are put. Diagnostic assessment is commonly developed and tested by others with the necessary resources and expertise. Formative and summative assessment are more common and largely the responsibility of the teacher. When assessment is devised for formative purposes, it is intended to inform next steps in teaching and learning. When assessment is devised for summative purposes, the outcomes are used as a summary of achievements to record and often to report to others who are unfamiliar with the course of learning. While any assessment can be used for formative or summative purposes, it will achieve its purpose more successfully if it has been created for that particular purpose.

5   Be clear about who you want to assess

This chapter is all about

- Devising assessment with particular students in mind
- Ensuring that none of those students are disadvantaged by your assessment
- Why inclusive assessment means better assessment for everyone

This short chapter won't take you long to read and you may feel the question is easy to answer. However, consideration of who is to be assessed is often skimmed over, but it is important for assessment quality. In addition to having a clear purpose, good educational assessment should always be devised with particular students in mind. We need to think carefully about which students we are devising assessment for to make sure that it suits them and doesn't exclude anyone unnecessarily.

Think of your students

It is obvious that assessment created for 7-year-olds will likely not be suitable for most 17-year-olds, but it's equally true that one created for 10-year-olds is unlikely to be optimal for 9-year-olds, or 10-year-olds with specific learning needs or 10-year-olds with gaps in their education.

An educational assessment might be intended for a particular class of students in a primary school or in a secondary school, an age group

Be clear about who you want to assess

across the whole country, a group of children with special educational needs, a cohort of adults, children in the pre-school age range, and so on. Good assessment is likely to look very different for each of these groups, so assessment should be designed with your target students in mind.

> The best assessment is created with your target students very clearly in mind.

That's not to say that there is any kind of direct relationship between age, level and type of educational assessment. Observation is commonly used to assess preschool children, bus drivers and trainee doctors, to name just a few! The important thing is to keep your target students clearly in mind and make sure your assessment is optimal for them. Good assessment should allow students in the target group to demonstrate *readily* what they know and can do, unimpeded by *irrelevant* challenges.

Make sure your assessment is for all of your students

Fairness and inclusion should be kept clearly in mind at every stage during your thinking about assessment. In Chapter 2, we discussed the qualities of all good assessment, and fairness is one of those key qualities. Good assessment should provide everyone with an equitable opportunity to show what they know and can do.

We need to think about all the ways in which some students might find it difficult to access an assessment. Many countries have laws that prohibit discrimination against individuals on the grounds of particular characteristics, including disabilities. But inclusive assessment should go beyond that to include a wide range of circumstances that might disadvantage students with less access to time, resources or experiences, or whose experiences might be very different to those of most other students.

Classroom Assessment for Teachers

We can't assume that all students have access to the same space, resources and support, so we must take steps to ensure that assessment doesn't require anything of students that *all* students may not have access to. For example, a student that has no study space or no IT facilities at home may find it difficult to show what they know and can do in parts of an assessment that are to be done there, as would students with caring responsibilities that take up much of their time. Assessment that assumes certain cultural norms and knowledge will disadvantage those whose cultures and norms are different. Inclusive assessment should try to accommodate all students.

> Inclusive assessment should consider *any* circumstances that might disadvantage particular students.

Keep these ideas in the front of your mind when devising classroom assessment for students you know well. That should help you to see how easy it would be to get assessment wrong for some students. It will help you to get assessment right for your students, and you can look out for these dangers when evaluating assessments that others have produced.

Whether the purpose of your assessment is formative or summative, it will likely work better if it is seen as being something done with your students rather than to them. If students can regard assessment as something to benefit them – an opportunity to show what they know and can do or to get feedback that will help them to learn better – they are likely to benefit more from it.

Finally, assessment that is tightly focused on exactly what evidence for assessment you really *need* will likely increase the fairness and inclusivity of that assessment and will provide more valid assessment for *everyone.*

Be clear about who you want to assess

> *Practical Step 2:*
> *Make sure your assessment is devised with your students in mind and is fair for all of your students, because inclusive assessment benefits everyone.*

Summary

In this very short chapter, we introduced the idea of devising assessment with particular students in mind. That's because assessment devised for particular students is likely to work better than assessment that is not. We also revisited the concepts of fairness and inclusion introduced in Chapter 2. We did this to emphasise that careful thought needs to be given to ensuring that *all* students can show what they know and can do. That means going beyond any legal requirements there might be and making sure that assessment doesn't require anything of students that all students may not have access to, such as cultural knowledge and experiences, time or other resources. Such a focus should help to ensure that assessment is devised to provide only essential evidence for assessment, which will itself contribute to assessment quality.

6 Be clear about what you want to assess

This chapter is all about

- The importance of having a very clear idea about what it is you want to assess
- The relationship between what you want to assess and the evidence for assessment you need
- Intended learning outcomes
- Assessment of abstract constructs
- Sharing the focus of assessment with students

In previous chapters, we thought about why you might want to assess and whom. We learned that every assessment should have a clear purpose because that will affect decisions about how best to go about it. It determines how often and when assessment is likely to happen, and how formal assessment is likely to be. It informs the kinds and amounts of evidence for assessment you are likely to need: whether that is evidence of what has been learned or evidence for what has not. And we touched on why it is important to devise your assessment with your intended students in mind. The next big question to ask yourself about your assessment is exactly *what* do you want to assess?

Be clear about what you want to assess

The focus of assessment

If you can get a sharp focus on what you want to assess early in your thinking about assessment, it can have a great impact on its validity. That's because what you want to assess will tell you exactly what evidence you need, and you can then devise assessment to provide exactly that! The focus for your assessment might be a particular area of new knowledge or skills, deeper knowledge or skills, increasing confidence in knowledge or skills or the application of knowledge or skills in new contexts. You might be looking for evidence of creativity or collaboration, perseverance or problem-solving. Whatever you're looking for evidence *of* will be the focus of your assessment, whatever its purpose.

> Being clear about what you want to assess will tell you exactly what evidence for assessment you need and what your assessment needs to provide.

Ask yourself, 'What do I want my students to show me they know and can do?' Once you have that clear in your mind, you can immediately think about what kinds and amounts of evidence for assessment you will want to gather or to use an assessment to generate, because one leads very naturally to the other. That assessment might happen during learning or after it. It may happen frequently or infrequently, and it may be more or less formal, for summative or formative purposes. In every case, you should be clear about what it is that you are assessing and so what evidence for that would look like.

For example, if you want to assess whether a student can make an omelette safely, you will want to see an omelette being made safely and will probably want to taste it, too! If you want to assess what a student knows about certain geological features, you will most likely want to read or hear a student's answers to questions on that subject (because questions are a very efficient way to test knowledge). If you want to know whether a student has developed the knowledge and skills to deal with a difficult customer, you will want to see that knowledge and those skills in effective action.

Your assessment should always align with your curriculum, whether your curriculum is defined in terms of product or process, and however it is expressed, in learning outcomes, topic areas or experiential statements. Whatever your curriculum, good assessment requires that you are clear about what you are assessing and, therefore, what evidence for assessment you really need.

Intended learning outcomes

If you are assessing for summative purposes at the end of a course or period of learning, you may already have an answer to the important question – 'What do I want to assess?' – or at least the start of an answer. That's because you will likely have asked yourself at the start of the day, block, term or semester, 'What do I want you to learn?' and your assessment should tell you to what extent that intended learning has happened.

> What you want students to learn leads very naturally to what you will want to assess.

If you have captured the answer to 'What do I want you to learn?' in intended learning outcomes or similar, that will be an excellent starting point for devising your assessment. Intended learning outcomes

Be clear about what you want to assess

will describe clearly what the student should know and be able to do at the end of a course of learning, and your assessment should simply look for evidence of that.

Intended learning outcomes can be articulated for short or long periods of learning. Communicated well, they can guide teaching and assessment and also be an important source of information for the student. Intended learning outcomes are often addressed to the student, using a phrase such as 'On completion of this module or course or unit of learning, *you* will be able to . . .'. Typically, each intended learning outcome focusses on an essential area of knowledge or skill so that there is no duplication across them. They can help to ensure that assessment is well-focused and efficient. Intended learning outcomes should be clear and concise. They should be reasonably short and direct, and they should use plain language that students will understand.

Action verbs

Action verbs can play an important role in intended learning outcomes and in assessment (where they are often called 'command verbs'). The action verb chosen for a learning outcome should communicate clearly to the student how they can show what they know and can do: they should 'make', 'analyse', 'prepare', 'explain', or 'decorate', for example. There are many different guides to action verbs for use in intended learning outcomes, based on different taxonomies and for different cognitive or skills domains. But remember that these are only guides. There is no fixed relationship between a particular action verb and level in any taxonomy or framework. Describing, explaining, building or organising something can be relatively straightforward or require deep knowledge or great skill.

One important thing to consider is that if you are using intended learning outcomes, then it may be helpful to use the same kinds of verbs in your assessment. We revisit this idea in Chapter 8, but in the meantime, for example, if your intended learning outcomes look like this . . .

Classroom Assessment for Teachers

At the end of this course of learning you should be able to

- Decorate a three-tier wedding cake to a professional standard
- Explain, using scientific terms, the role of plants in photosynthesis
- Prepare a business plan suitable for a start-up company seeking a business loan

Your evidence for assessment is likely to be this!

- A three-tier wedding cake decorated to a professional standard
- An explanation, using scientific terms, of the role of plants in photosynthesis
- A business plan suitable for a start-up company seeking a business loan

Assessment of abstract constructs

In education, most often, what you need to know is whether or to what extent a student knows something or can do something. Some things that you might want to assess will be fairly familiar: knowledge and skills in the subjects or areas of learning that you've been teaching for some time. But what if you want to assess something that is not part of the knowledge and skills of a particular discipline? These might be cross-disciplinary skills like creativity or problem-solving or the attributes that education increasingly seeks to develop, like resilience. Can those be assessed? The answer is, 'Yes!' It can be argued that the process of devising suitable assessment for anything will help us to understand what that thing really *is*.

Unlike physical characteristics that we can readily measure or estimate like height and weight, tricky things like confidence, creativity, perseverance and resilience can't be seen. They exist only as 'abstract constructs'. Abstract constructs are things that we can't directly observe but we may be able to describe, especially through exploring, discussing and reaching agreement with others about exactly what we think those things are. It can be argued that knowledge and skills are also abstract constructs, and we have been confidently assessing those for

Be clear about what you want to assess

hundreds of years! Exactly what *is* 'knowledge'? Memorisation? Or more than that? What *is* 'understanding', and how does that relate to knowledge? What exactly are the skills of a mathematician, a joiner, a doctor, an artist, an early reader?

> Working with others, the nature of an abstract construct can be defined, and evidence for assessment of that construct can then be identified.

In each case, assessment is based on identifying as clearly as possible what is relevant and what is not relevant to assessment of that construct. There is no reason to believe that we can't assess other abstract constructs in education. It may be challenging, but it's certainly possible, and it is done in many other measurement fields. Valid and reliable instruments to measure tricky things like brand loyalty or customer satisfaction, quality of life or ethical reasoning are just a few examples of abstract constructs that are seen as valuable and, sometimes, essential to measure. Whether you want to assess customer satisfaction or creativity, the critical first step in devising assessment of an abstract construct is to define or clearly describe exactly what that thing *is*. Once that is done, the next step is to explore and agree upon what the signs of this are likely to be, and there are many steps after that.

Even the first step requires a highly collaborative approach among those with relevant expertise and experience. Exactly what *is* creativity, what *is* problem-solving, what *is* resilience? Once that is clear in your mind – and especially if you can arrive at that understanding after discussion with colleagues – you can begin to identify what evidence of it would look like. If creativity is *this*, then signs of creativity will be *those*, and assessment should be devised to obtain and judge evidence of exactly those things. Any more on this is well beyond the scope of this book. For now, we hope it is helpful to know that it almost certainly can be done and encourage you to explore existing assessments for such abstract constructs and build upon the work that is increasingly being undertaken in this field.

You can see that the question 'Exactly what do you want to assess?' may not be as simple as it seems. But it is important to try to have a very clear idea about your focus for assessment – what it *is* and *what evidence of that will be* – upon which all later decisions about your assessment will rest. You may want to assess across a breadth of knowledge and skills or your focus may be quite narrow. Whatever you want to assess, it is very important to have that clear in your mind from the outset and throughout the process of devising good assessment for your students.

> All decisions about assessment should relate to *exactly* what it is that you want to assess.

So, don't rush your thinking at this point. Be very clear about what you want to assess and what evidence of that will look like. This is critical for valid assessment. Get it wrong and there will be little you can do later to put your assessment right. When you think this is clear in your head, you might want to write it down, but don't be afraid to go back and tweak it if you need to. Being clear in your mind about exactly what you want to assess will be your touchstone throughout all the stages of devising or creating good assessment.

> Valid assessment begins with a very clear idea of what you want to assess and what evidence of that will look like.

Be clear about what you want to assess

If you have time, you may wish to discuss your assessment focus with colleagues and ask them to be critical friends. They may be subject experts or not. Subject experts bring valuable expertise and experience to the discussion about assessment focus. Colleagues that don't have expertise in a subject can offer a very valuable perspective that may be more closely aligned with that of your students, and that can be very helpful as well.

Share your assessment focus with your students

Ethically, as well as for assessment validity, your students should be clear about what you will be looking for while they are learning and preparing for assessment. For assessment of school-age students, it would be good practice to make sure that those who support them know what is being assessed, too. It can be a very useful check to ask yourself, 'Will my students easily understand what I'm looking for . . . and would their grandmothers?'

> Ethically, as well as for assessment validity, students should be clear about what you are looking for while preparing for assessment or being assessed.

Whatever your approach to curriculum, learning is most effective when a student is engaged in their own learning journey, and effective assessment is part of that learning journey. Good assessment will facilitate and value that engagement in assessment linked to learning. Discussing with students what *they* are aiming for – what success will look and feel like to *them* – is just one way in which students can be more fully engaged in their own assessment. Discussion with students about how they hope to develop and over what period of time and what evidence of that development might look like can strongly motivate learning. Making sure that assessment is

Classroom Assessment for Teachers

completely aligned with those shared expectations and involving the student in identifying evidence for assessment are powerful ways of making assessment a positive and effective experience for students. For good assessment, your students should be very clear about what they are aiming for.

> Students can be partners in good assessment, which should make it as positive an experience as possible for them.

If the focus of your assessment is clear to you, it can also be made clear to your students: as a result, they will be much more likely to succeed!

> **Practical Step 3:**
> *Be very clear about what it is that you want to assess so that you can devise your assessment to obtain evidence of exactly that.*

Summary

In this chapter, we discussed the importance of clearly defining what you want to assess, since that will determine the evidence for assessment you need to obtain. For example, if you use intended learning outcomes or similar, which describe clearly what you expect your students to learn and how they can demonstrate that, then the evidence you need for assessment should be very clear. While most assessments focus on knowledge or skills, there is growing interest in assessing abstract constructs like creativity and resilience.

Be clear about what you want to assess

Although challenging, assessment should be possible though defining the construct and thus identifying relevant evidence for assessment. Whatever and however you are assessing, it is important to make expectations clear to students. Not only should this improve the quality of assessment, it should engage students and help make assessment a positive part of their learning journey.

Choose approaches and methods to suit your purpose and the evidence for assessment you need

This chapter is all about

- Why we need just enough of the right kinds of evidence for assessment
- Deciding whether evidence for assessment can be gathered or should be generated using an assessment task
- Choosing methods of assessment that suit the kinds of evidence for assessment you need
- Authentic assessment
- What 'tests and exams' are good for and what they are not

Once you are clear about who and why you are assessing and exactly what you want to assess, you can more clearly think about the best way to do that. What kinds of evidence for assessment do you need? What method of assessment will be best for that? Is that evidence likely to occur naturally or will you need to use an assessment task to generate it? These will be really important decisions for assessment validity and will be the focus of this chapter.

Good assessment comes from keeping a focus on . . .

- What students are expected to know and be able to do, which tells you . . .

DOI: 10.4324/9781003564478-10

Choose approaches and methods to suit your purpose

- What evidence for assessment you need, and that informs decisions about . . .
- How that evidence can best be obtained

Evidence for assessment should be relevant and adequate

Evidence for assessment can take many different forms – it might be ephemeral or physical, a process or a product, evidence of knowledge or skills of many different kinds. You will want to be sure to choose an approach to assessment that is most likely to provide you with the kind and amount of evidence you need. That choice will contribute in a very significant way to the validity of your assessment. Good assessment should be based upon evidence for assessment that is entirely relevant and adequate for what and why you want to assess.

> Good assessment will provide evidence that is relevant and adequate for your assessment purpose and focus.

Let's consider an example. It may seem obvious that evidence for the knowledge and skills required to bake a cake can best be obtained by asking the student to bake a cake rather than to write an essay about how to bake a cake, but it can be helpful to think about *why* that is. Any good assessment should produce evidence that is entirely *relevant* and *adequate* for what you mean to assess. Writing an essay about how to bake a cake provides evidence for essay-writing skills, but these are not *relevant* to the skills of cake baking. The essay could provide evidence for *relevant* knowledge about how to bake a cake, but unless the student does actually bake the cake, we don't have *adequate* evidence for assessment of those cake-baking skills.

Classroom Assessment for Teachers

That very simple example shows the importance of thinking about how best to go about gathering or generating evidence for your assessment that is both relevant and adequate. Gather or generate the wrong kind of evidence or not enough of the right kind of evidence and your assessment will not be as valid as it would be if you were able to gather or generate just enough evidence of exactly the right kind.

There are two main ways to obtain evidence for assessment. It can be gathered as it occurs naturally during learning, or it can be deliberately generated using an assessment task of some kind.

> The right kind and amount of evidence for assessment could be gathered during learning or might need to be generated using an assessment task.

Gathering evidence for assessment

You may be able to gather evidence for assessment in the course of your students' learning, which is likely to be more efficient than using assessment tasks to generate it. This approach will be especially useful when assessment is to be used for formative purposes, because it will be completely integrated into the day-to-day activities of the classroom and the outcomes can be used immediately to adjust teaching and learning as required. Gathering naturally occurring evidence is not a method of assessment, but rather it is an approach to assessment that could use a number of different methods. For example, you might gather naturally occurring evidence for assessment using observation, by assessing written work or by asking questions orally. Once you have determined what kind of evidence you need and how much, you may find that adequate and relevant evidence is likely to be produced naturally in the course of learning. All you then need to do is judge that evidence and use its outcomes for your intended purpose.

Choose approaches and methods to suit your purpose

Generating evidence for assessment

If you need to *generate* evidence for assessment, rather than gather it as it occurs naturally, then you will need to use an assessment task of some kind. An assessment task is a set of instructions that tell students what they need to do to generate the evidence for assessment that you need. That might be a test or exam made up of questions that require one-word answers or much longer responses. It could be a project that offers an issue to research, or it could be a creative task with a brief to address. It could be oral instructions such as those given by a driving assessor, or it could be the clear requirement in a medical assessment to make a diagnosis from symptoms described by an actor playing the part of a patient.

> An assessment task helps students to provide the evidence you need by giving them clear instructions about what you want them to do.

The job of the assessment task is to help the student produce the evidence you need as directly and efficiently as possible. What kind of task would help your students to provide you with the right kind and amount of evidence for assessment as directly and efficiently as possible? That will depend on the nature of the evidence you need. Is it going to be ephemeral or physical? A process or a product? Evidence of what kinds of knowledge or what sorts of skills? To generate that evidence, will you ask your students to respond to questions? To make something? To demonstrate their skills in dance, drama or sport? To respond to a real-life simulation? To research a topic or respond to a design brief over an extended period of time?

These questions don't define particular methods of assessment, and they are not mutually exclusive – you may find yourself answering 'yes' to two or more of them. But thinking about the nature of the evidence for assessment you need and the kinds of tasks you might use to generate it will guide you to the best method or methods for valid assessment of what you want to assess.

> The job of any assessment task is to help the student produce the evidence you need as directly and efficiently as possible.

There is no end to the ways in which you can generate evidence for assessment. Even formal assessment of the kind used for many sorts of national or state certificates will probably make use of a wide range of assessment methods including performances, products, written and oral examinations, projects, dissertations, and portfolios. In your own classroom, the only limit is your imagination! However, what is most important is that the method of assessment you choose should allow you to generate *just enough* of the *right kind* of evidence. This will help ensure that your assessment is valid and as fair and practical as possible for your students.

Methods of assessment

Whether evidence for assessment is obtained naturally in the course of learning or is generated using an assessment task, it should always suit the focus of your assessment. Questioning is the most efficient and straightforward way to assess knowledge and some cognitive skills, but to assess practical skills, you will likely want evidence in the form of a product or performance. For example, if you want to assess cake-baking skills, ask the student to bake a cake and judge the quality of their finished product (and perhaps the safety and efficiency of the process they used to produce it). If you want to assess research skills, ask your students to carry out a research project. If you want to assess drawing and painting skills, ask your students to draw and paint a variety

Choose approaches and methods to suit your purpose

of subjects and gather their work in a portfolio. If you want to assess whether your students can respond appropriately to an emergency in a healthcare setting, then set up a simulation and tell them the role that they must play within it. The method of assessment should suit the *kind* of evidence for assessment you need.

> Methods of assessment should be carefully chosen to provide the kinds of evidence for assessment you need as directly and efficiently as possible.

Where assessment methods relate to assessment tasks, they can have different names in different assessment systems, and, indeed, the same name can be used with different meanings in different systems. Check what guidance is available in your local context. For example, in some assessment systems everything that involves the student speaking is called an 'oral test'. In other assessment systems, everything that involves the student speaking is called a 'performance assessment'. Next, we provide some examples of assessment methods as we would describe them, each illustrated by the kinds of assessment tasks we might include in those categories.

An **oral method of assessment** might take the form of

- Oral questions that assess knowledge and understanding and may be linked to the assessment of a practical activity or performance
- An oral test of a student's listening and communication skills in their own or a learned language
- A conversation with a teacher or assessor that aims to capture the student's speaking skills in their own or a learned language
- A professional discussion of a workplace scenario to assess knowledge of how to deal with situations that the student did not encounter in practice

Classroom Assessment for Teachers

A **performance method of assessment** might take the form of

- A dramatic or dance performance, solo or in groups, to you or a wider audience
- A sporting performance, solo or in groups, in conditions that are as realistic as possible for how that sport is usually played
- A workplace performance, in a real or simulated situation, in which the student demonstrates their ability to deal with a particular scenario, such as a receptionist dealing with an awkward visitor

A **practical method of assessment** might take the form of

- Producing a dish or meal to a defined specification and within a set period of time
- Carrying out a scientific experiment
- Over a longer period, making something in hard materials (such as wood, metal or plastic) to a defined specification
- Creating a media artefact to meet a given client brief
- Building a wall

A **project method of assessment** might take the form of

- An investigation, dissertation or research project, with a defined research question, a choice of selected research questions, or a free choice of questions to investigate and report on
- An assignment that is more structured, perhaps assessing problem-solving, and with clear guidelines on structure and length
- A case study in which a realistic situation is presented to the student in some detail, with the requirement to analyse the situation, draw conclusions/make decisions/suggest courses of action

A **portfolio method of assessment** might take the form of

- Pieces of evidence collected over time intended to represent the student's best and/or latest work

Choose approaches and methods to suit your purpose

- Pieces of evidence collected over time intended to be a representative sample of the student's work over a course of learning
- Pieces of evidence chosen freely by the student

A **test or exam** might take the form of

- A written test, consisting of a collection of questions that sample a particular area of knowledge and/or skills
- An aural test which assesses listening skills using a live or recorded stimulus to which responses might be written or oral
- One or more of the listed methods of assessment but to be carried out under exam conditions: on a single occasion, within a defined timeframe, with access only to specified resources, and with no conferring allowed

Using more than one method of assessment

The method of assessment should be chosen to suit the kind of evidence for assessment you need, and you might choose to use more than one method if you need different kinds of evidence. For example, you might want to use a practical assessment to gather evidence of practical skills and also to ask questions to test related knowledge. You might want to evaluate a product but be equally interested to observe the process that led to it. For example, if assessing student chefs, you may want to assess the quality of the dishes they produce and also whether their practices meet health and safety requirements and whether they know what to do in the case of a kitchen fire, for example. Not only could using more than one method of assessment make your assessment more valid, it might also make it more inclusive and fair. Some students may perform better with one method of assessment than the other, so using more than one method could allow students different opportunities to show best what they know and can do.

Authentic assessment

There is some debate about exactly what 'authentic assessment' is. It can be generally understood to be assessment conducted through tasks that ask students to show what they know and can do in meaningful contexts. Those contexts might be real-world situations or problems including those that call for subject- or discipline-specific practices. Authentic assessment tends to be integrated with learning or work.

Authentic assessment is believed to be more engaging for students because they can more easily see the relevance of the assessment tasks. It can build confidence, offer a degree of personalisation, and offer a more valid approach to assessment of particular kinds of knowledge, skills and competences. But it can also be challenging for both students and teachers. Just as with any other kind of assessment, teachers can create authentic assessments by devising appropriate approaches or tasks and instructions for judging the evidence students will produce.

For validity, students should always know when they are being assessed. If evidence is being gathered during learning, they should know that anything they do during that learning might be used as evidence for assessment. If students are clear about what is being assessed, then they should be able to have confidence that assessment will be devised to gather (and reward) evidence of exactly that. The qualities of authentic assessment should be the same as for any other kind of assessment – it should be valid, reliable, fair and practical.

> For assessment validity, students should always know when they are being assessed or when what they are doing could be used as evidence for assessment.

Tests and exams

In common usage, the word 'test' means something much broader than sitting down at a desk to answer some questions on a piece of paper. Resisting that second piece of chocolate cake is definitely a test of willpower for some of us! And many situations in life can test our patience

Choose approaches and methods to suit your purpose

or resilience. We can easily recognise and use that everyday sense of the word 'test'.

'Examination' doesn't have quite such a broad meaning in common usage, but it can have different meanings in different assessment systems. In some assessment systems, any assessment at the end of a course of learning and with some degree of formality will be called an 'exam'. In others, the word 'exam' is only used for sit-down, pen-and-paper tests taken under strict conditions. In this section of the chapter, we want to reflect in a bit more depth about that more limited definition of tests and exams – the sit-down (usually pen-and-paper) test, taken under defined and often quite strict conditions. We reflect on those here, not because they are more important than any other assessment method, but because they are often the most commonly used assessment method – and the most frequently criticised!

What's good about tests and exams?

Tests and exams, whether written or oral, are usually made up of a collection of items. Assessment items might be questions or something else that students need to respond to. They might require the student to respond in different ways: by ticking a box, by selecting the right answer, by writing a short response or by composing a paragraph or longer essay. They can also include mini-versions of some of the assessment methods that we've described as alternatives to tests and exams. A test or exam could include a short case study, for example. In all of these instances, the test or exam is likely to contain a number of assessment items although it could be just one.

Tests and exams give the teacher or assessor an opportunity to ask a range of questions in one assessment. Questioning is a very direct and efficient way to obtain evidence of someone's knowledge. If you want to know what someone knows, ask them! One way that an exam can do this efficiently is by sampling from all of the knowledge you expect the student to know. If you want to know that I have memorised a body of knowledge, then you can ask me about part of it and may be able to infer from my knowledge of those parts that I probably know the rest, too. In the case of an exam where I have not seen the questions in advance, I will have had to learn the whole course in order to be confident that I can answer any question that might be asked. Sampling means that assessment can be more efficient, which is good for both student and assessor. There is no rule about how much of a sample you need to take to be able to infer other knowledge – that is a judgement for you or for any assessment professional.

> Questioning is a very direct and efficient way to obtain evidence of someone's knowledge, especially when we can sample from a wider body of knowledge.

Questions can be asked orally or you can use some kind of written test. A written test that many students can respond to at the same time can be much more efficient than asking questions orally of individual students although sometimes the latter is more effective. The consequences of such tests can be significant (in the case of assessments for national qualifications, for example) or quite small (in the case of end-of-topic quizzes).

We've talked a lot about knowledge in this section, but tests and exams are not just good for assessing what students know and can remember. You can also use them to assess cognitive skills like analysing, evaluating and solving problems. Tests and exams are certainly a valuable approach to consider for the assessment of some of the things you may want to assess, and in many instances they will provide you with an efficient way to generate just enough of the kinds of evidence you need.

Choose approaches and methods to suit your purpose

What's the problem with tests and exams?

We've noted already that tests and exams are probably the most common (and almost certainly the oldest) method of assessment, but they are also the most frequently and heavily criticised. You may work in an assessment system where tests and exams are rarely used, and a range of other assessment methods are valued. You might work in a system where only tests and exams are used, and no other assessment method is seen as reliable and credible. Or, like us, you may have experienced assessment systems where the issue of whether tests and exams represent 'good' or 'bad' assessment is one that is hotly debated. Whatever your situation, you may find it helpful to think in a bit more depth about criticisms of tests and exams and whether these are justified.

Perhaps the most common criticism of tests and exams is that they encourage 'teaching to the test' by rewarding memorisation and rote learning rather than deep learning. That may be true, but it is also true, as we noted before, that tests and exams can assess higher order cognitive skills like reasoning, analysis and problem solving.

Another criticism of tests and exams can occur when they are used to assess practical skills that (perhaps arguably) cannot be validly assessed by a test or exam. An exam can be used to assess whether a student knows how to set up scientific apparatus, but it can't tell us anything about whether they can actually do that in practice. On the other hand, a practical assessment of the student's ability to set up apparatus and carry out an experiment may not provide any evidence that they could carry out a different type of experiment, deal with any shortcomings in their apparatus or solve problems with the apparatus. If we are going to assess that kind of underpinning knowledge, we will probably need to use questioning of some sort (or add in multiple practical assessments that are going to take hours to conduct). Questioning to establish underpinning knowledge can take place orally, or it can be done efficiently using a written test.

Classroom Assessment for Teachers

There are, of course, other important criticisms of tests and exams; for example, they demotivate those who do not do well by labelling them 'failures', they happen on a single day and if students 'have a bad day' they may be judged on a performance that does not really reflect what they know and can do, and they cause anxiety and stress even for younger pupils. As in any debate, there is some truth to all of these criticisms, but there are also counter-arguments and no simple answer.

Finally, we mustn't forget that some students cannot read or write, for example, pre-school learners and older students with specific learning needs. Thinking about assessment for such students can be a useful way to find a fresh perspective on educational assessment, since traditional, written tests and exams just won't allow some students to show what they know and can do.

All assessment methods have strengths and weaknesses

Not only are there counter-arguments to every criticism of tests and exams, but every assessment method has strengths and weaknesses. Every method will be useful for a different purpose, in a different context, to assess a different set of knowledge and skills, with different students.

For example, portfolios of evidence for different students might include a great assortment of pieces of evidence giving you the job of 'comparing apples and oranges' and making it difficult for you to be sure that you are judging evidence reliably and fairly. Some students report that knowing that any piece of work might go into their assessment portfolio means that they feel they are constantly under stress, can never relax and enjoy their learning, and are always under pressure to 'do their best'. This might even discourage them from trying out new things, using trial and error, and taking risks – and thus is lost a very important part of learning. We could create a long list of the strengths and weaknesses of each assessment method. There is no space to do that in this short guide, but we encourage you to thoughtfully select different methods of assessment and discover these for yourself.

Choose approaches and methods to suit your purpose

What we hope we have provided, instead, is advice that will help you make good choices of methods that will begin to establish the validity of your assessment – that will provide you with the right kinds of evidence for the kinds of learning you want to assess. In some instances, tests and exams will come out as the best method to use. In other cases, another method will offer more advantages. Each has strengths, and each has important drawbacks. Your job is to decide on the right method for what you want your assessment to do.

> **Practical Step 4:**
> Choose assessment approaches and methods that will most directly and efficiently provide you with the kinds of evidence for assessment you need.

Summary

In this chapter, we explained that what students are expected to know and be able to do tells you what evidence for assessment you need which in turn informs decisions about how such evidence can best be obtained. Evidence for assessment should be relevant and adequate for the purpose and the focus of your assessment. It can be gathered as it occurs naturally, in the course of learning, or it can be generated using an assessment task. There are broad methods of assessment that can be applied to obtaining any evidence for assessment, including evidence produced during authentic assessment. The method or methods chosen, whether evidence is to be gathered or generated, should most directly and efficiently provide the evidence for assessment that you need. Tests and exams are commonly used for assessment, and they come with advantages but also disadvantages and so must be used thoughtfully. They are just one option and others may be better for your purpose and the focus of your assessment.

8 Create assessment tasks that help students produce the evidence for assessment you need

This chapter is all about

- Creating 'a test worth teaching to'
- Using the right kind of task or item to provide the evidence for assessment you need
- Communicating the task to students
- Avoiding potential pitfalls in assessment tasks
- Avoiding assessment drift
- Assessment context and conditions of assessment
- Assessment efficiency

So, you've decided upon the purpose and focus for your assessment and the kind of evidence for assessment you're looking for, and you've made some big decisions about methods of assessment to best provide that evidence. But if you are creating an assessment task there are still lots more decisions to be made! Each one of those smaller decisions can maintain or could undermine the quality of your assessment.

Remember, good assessment comes from keeping a focus on . . .

- what students are expected to know and be able to do, which tells you . . .
- what evidence for assessment you need, and therefore . . .
- how that evidence can best be obtained

Create assessment tasks that produce the evidence you need

A test worth teaching to

Teachers who want their students to do well in tests will prepare them for that test as well as they can, so any assessment task is likely to have a strong washback effect on what is taught and learned. Research shows that teachers have strong views on the sorts of washback effects that assessment can have. Some believe that assessment can help boost learning by motivating students to do their best, either through a wish for reward or a fear of failure. Others believe that too sharp a focus on assessment outcomes, especially of assessment for summative purposes, can have a negative effect on learning. They can narrow what teachers teach and what students are motivated to learn – reducing classroom activity to 'teaching to the test'. The counter argument to that is that those devising assessments should ensure that they create a test worth teaching to! A good test is one that is absolutely aligned with the knowledge and skills you hope to develop and are looking for evidence of, that generates the right kind of evidence as directly and efficiently as possible, and that judges that evidence in the right way. That is going to be a test worth teaching to.

> A 'test worth teaching to' is one that is aligned with what and how students are expected to learn.

Different kinds of assessment task or item

The job of an assessment task is to generate exactly the kinds and also the amounts of evidence for assessment that you need. What kind of student response will provide that kind of evidence? Are you looking for evidence that something has been learned or not, such as knowledge of a particular fact? Or, are you looking for evidence for knowledge or skills that can't be provided in a simple, right or wrong answer? Are you assessing knowledge or skills that your students may demonstrate in different amounts, with some students demonstrating great breadth or depth and others demonstrating less breadth or depth? What kind of task or item will best allow students to produce the kind of evidence you need? How much of that evidence do you need to generate?

> The assessment task or item should suit the kind and amount of evidence you need.

It is useful to think of assessment tasks being broken down into 'items'. These items might take the form of a question or they may be instructions of some kind. In some instances, your assessment task may contain just one item but usually more. We are going to provide some broad explanations of the main assessment item types. We have chosen to use broad/general terms for these. While the terms we use might differ somewhat from those used in your own assessment system, you should recognise these item types, and our advice should help you to select which type to use and how to use each well. Our suggestions will help you mainly with devising assessment items for written assessment tasks, but some of them will also be useful when you are devising other kinds of task.

Assessment items with a correct answer

These are items that will simply show that a student knows something, or knows how to do something, or does not. Such assessment items have an objectively correct answer. They can take a range of forms according to the knowledge and skills being assessed. They could be multiple choice or fill-in-the-blank items. They might be instructions to carry out a computation or to identify a fault in a piece of machinery. The important thing is that the item should most directly and efficiently allow you to know if the student knows something, or knows how to do something, or not. Often, the student doesn't have to come up with the answer themselves, but

Create assessment tasks that produce the evidence you need

instead, they have to recognise or choose the right answer from options given. In assessment jargon, this item type is sometimes known as an objective-type item because there is just one objectively correct answer.

One well-known objective-type item is the multiple-choice item. You will see them every time you fill in a market research survey or take a magazine or online quiz. A multiple-choice item is made up of a question, or sometimes a statement, followed by usually four or five possible answers from which to choose, only one of which is correct. This type of item allows you to generate evidence of knowledge and some cognitive skills with very little writing required of the student. All the student needs to do is tick or circle the correct answer or, perhaps, write the letter corresponding to the right answer into an answer grid.

Similar item types might ask the student to match pairs of answers. You may be familiar with this sort of assessment item from online language learning apps. Or a range of statements may be given, and the student has to say whether each one is true or false. Or students may be given a list of words to insert into a short passage that has gaps left in it. All of these item types are relatively straightforward for the student to complete, and they have the advantage that they don't require the student to write much, if anything. They can also be marked very easily and reliably. They do take a little time and effort to create, however.

Assessment items where the student has to select a response rather than come up with one for themselves can be an efficient and not too stressful way for you to assess a lot of knowledge in a relatively short assessment. But they are not just useful for assessing knowledge, they can also be used to assess a range of cognitive skills like reasoning, and analysis of a passage of text or a diagram. We shouldn't assume that they are only useful at lower levels of learning, either: they can be used to assess skills and knowledge at the highest levels. They are commonly used in medical training in higher education, for example.

While it's possible for evidence to show whether many kinds of knowledge and skills are simply there or not, this kind of item is going to be of most use to you in assessment of knowledge and, especially, if your assessment method is a written test or exam. You can put together a whole test using such items, or you can include some at the start of your test. Here, they may help to settle your students' test nerves, as students may be able to answer them relatively quickly and build a little bit of confidence.

But these kinds of items don't need to be in a written format. You could use them in any assessment task that involves some questioning, including oral assessments. Here they may be useful to help you quickly check your students' underpinning knowledge when they have carried out a performance or practical assessment.

Another type of assessment item that may have an objectively correct answer is the short-answer item. These are exactly what they sound like. This type of question is a bit like a television quiz: 'Fingers on the buzzers now ... Name three ingredients you need to make a cake!' The short answers required can be a word, a phrase, a sentence, or even a few sentences. How these differ from things like multiple-choice items is that the student needs to supply the answer for themselves rather than selecting it from a number of possible answers provided. Short-answer items may use only words but can also use diagrams, graphs or numbers. The shortest of short-answer items, requiring only a word or two in response or a label to be added to a diagram, will almost certainly have objectively right and wrong answers.

Short-answer items are very familiar in educational assessment. They are commonly used as part of day-to-day informal assessment as well as in periodic, more formal assessments. While they are often put together into tests or exams, short-answer items probably have a role to play alongside most assessment methods and as part of most assessment occasions. They can be useful when you want to put together a test to assess a body of knowledge. They can also be relatively straightforward and quick to mark. As part of many kinds of assessment, at all stages of learning and in all subjects, they are probably the teacher's main way of quickly checking knowledge and understanding.

Create assessment tasks that produce the evidence you need

Short-answer items might simply ask the student to state, name or describe something, but they can also require the student to reason, apply knowledge, or solve problems that require a short response! In science, engineering or other practical subjects, for example, you might supply a diagram of a piece of equipment and simply ask the student to name or label the parts of the apparatus. To assess more complex reasoning, you might ask the student to say what would happen if a particular change was made to the apparatus (and this could be done orally or in writing). Whatever the requirements, if the student response is likely to have simply a right or wrong answer, then this is an objective-type item designed to obtain evidence that the student simply knows or can do something, or does not.

Items intended to elicit a range of acceptable responses or evidence of particular kinds

Some kinds of assessment items are not designed to elicit an objectively correct or incorrect response. Instead, the assessment task or item is intended to help students provide evidence of certain kinds of learning that can only be demonstrated in an extended response of some kind or to demonstrate *different amounts* of knowledge or skills. A variety or range of responses to an assessment task or item are expected, and the instructions for marking or judging such tasks or items need to allow for these different responses, all of which could be acceptable and worthy of credit to different degrees. The job of these items is to allow students to respond in this way, and so give you the evidence you need.

> Assessment tasks or items should allow students to respond in the ways that will most directly and efficiently give you the kinds and amounts of evidence for assessment you need.

Classroom Assessment for Teachers

This category of item types can include some short-answer items. If the short answer required is a phrase, a sentence, or more than one sentence, then we are starting to introduce the potential for more than one possible answer to be acceptable, and instructions for marking or judging your student's responses will have to ensure that they have taken account of all possible answers. We will look in more detail at how to devise instructions for judging evidence for assessment in the next chapter. Here, we are more interested in the idea of devising tasks or items that will best suit the kinds of evidence for assessment that we need – in this case, evidence that demonstrates certain kinds of learning or where students are likely to demonstrate different amounts of knowledge or skills.

The items that we most often think of when we imagine assessment intended to elicit a variety or range of acceptable responses are at the other end of the spectrum from objective-type assessment items, certainly in terms of the length of response expected. They would include, for example, the sorts of items that require students to pull different kinds of knowledge together, apply it in new contexts, and perhaps to analyse or evaluate it in some depth. Or such items may ask your students to demonstrate a range of skills or to draw on their knowledge and skills to create something new. In tests and exams, such items might require students to write an essay or other extended response. They can also be found in project or research type assessments, where the evidence for assessment could be a report, dissertation or even a thesis. But it is not just written assessment items that can have a range of acceptable responses. This category also includes assessment items where the student response is not written but oral or where it is of an artistic or sporting performance, or the creation of a product such as a celebration cake!

Some people believe that such assessment items are the best or even the only way to assess more complex cognitive skills. It is true that they are useful if you want to assess your students' ability to select from their body of knowledge and put together a reasoned and justified argument.

Create assessment tasks that produce the evidence you need

They can also provide a bit of flexibility for your students: depending on how you phrase your item, students may be able to choose which particular topic or issue, or aspect of a topic or issue, they research or write about. In some subjects, you can also use these kinds of items to assess creative thinking or originality. However, it is certainly not necessary to use such items or tasks just because the assessment is for a more challenging course of learning. The most sophisticated ideas can be assessed using multiple-choice items! Extended response items should only be used if they are *the most direct and efficient* way to generate the evidence for assessment you need.

> Item types should be chosen only on the basis that they will most directly and efficiently generate the kinds and amounts of evidence you need.

You might think that it is easy to write a good assessment item of this type, but it is important that your question or instructions help steer your students very clearly in the right direction. You will want to provide a very clear indication of the sorts of skills and knowledge that you want your students to show you. You will also want to let your students know (in broad terms at least) how you will judge their responses. If you do not, your assessment is likely to be seen as unfair by at least some of your students and is likely to be less reliable and less valid, too.

Communication and common problems with assessment tasks

In the next part of this chapter, we will highlight the importance of communication and some things that need careful consideration if you are creating an assessment task for your students: command verbs; use of contexts and illustrations; and optional items and scaffolding. Some important things to think about, and some pitfalls to avoid!

Classroom Assessment for Teachers

Communication

Whatever your chosen method of assessment, task or item type, the clarity of your instructions to students is critical. Good assessment depends on everyone understanding what they need to do. The main job of any assessment task or item is to communicate clearly to students what they need to do to produce the evidence required (and to communicate clearly to assessors how to judge or mark that evidence, as we shall see in Chapter 9). For assessment validity, students should also know how their work will be judged while they prepare for it. Any lack of clarity for students means that they may not be directed to produce the evidence you're looking for and that you want to reward, and that will undermine the validity of your assessment.

> The main job of any assessment task or item is to communicate clearly to students what they need to do to produce the evidence you're looking for.

If you are creating an assessment task or item, it is good practice to test it out to make sure that it is clear to those it is intended for and helps them to provide the evidence you need.

Command verbs

'Command verbs' tell students what they need to do in an assessment. Whatever form your assessment task or item may take, your command verb should give the student a very clear idea of what sort of evidence you are looking for. For example, 'name' or 'describe' tells students to do something different than 'explain' or 'justify', 'plan' means something other than 'make' or 'evaluate'. Try to be thoughtful in how you do this and use command verbs in ways that are as close as possible to how those verbs are used in everyday language in your part of the

Create assessment tasks that produce the evidence you need

world. Students shouldn't have to learn a special language to know what an assessment item is asking them to do.

> Good assessment shouldn't need students to learn a special language in order to know what they are being asked to do.

Your command verbs should be appropriate for the task and the age and level of your students. It would be unreasonable, for example, to ask a very young student to 'justify' a choice that they had made! But don't assume that command verbs have a direct relationship with the level of a course of learning. At different levels, it may be reasonable and necessary to ask students to explain something very simple or something quite complex.

Using context in assessment tasks and items

There are many ways to confuse both students and markers, and these are especially obvious in the case of written assessments. For example, there are well-documented problems with using context in items. Not only can some contexts be unhelpful to students not familiar with them, they may actually be confusing, upsetting or even offensive. Contexts involving sports, holidays, foods, leisure activities and family roles could all exclude some students who have limited financial resources, who have disabilities, require particular diets, or are looked after or in care. The context or image of what is considered to be a 'family' in a particular culture may be completely irrelevant to many students and confusing or even upsetting to some. By their nature, contexts bring in culturally specific assumptions, and we must be particularly thoughtful when it comes to bringing these into assessment.

Here's an example of context being used in a test of arithmetic and causing confusion by adding extra detail that isn't needed:

> '*Travel With Us*' has small buses that can carry 28 passengers. A school is taking two groups of 8-year-olds to the museum. There are 14 children in one group and 15 in the other. Will they all fit on one bus?'

The context has irrelevant information like the name of the bus company, the purpose of the bus journey and the age of the pupils. Consequently, the item is testing a range of other things as well as arithmetic, such as reading skills, working memory, and problem-solving skills. If what you really want to know is whether or not a student knows how to add 14 and 15, just ask that!

Not only can contexts create confusion and additional difficulties for the student, first-hand experience of the context might advantage or disadvantage some students leading to an unfair assessment. For example, the context of a holiday might be unfamiliar to some students and, therefore, confuse or otherwise disadvantage them. The context of a hospital might be all too familiar to some students and cause an emotional reaction that would disadvantage them in an assessment. Asking students to put themselves into a situation *unnecessarily* is taking a risk that is better avoided.

This applies even when the context is one that you would be comfortable talking about as part of your classroom learning. In an assessment situation, students may already be feeling nervous or more sensitive, especially if the assessment is high stakes. In the classroom, you can make sure that sensitive topics are dealt with diplomatically, and you can look out for and support students who appear to be upset or offended. In an assessment situation, that is often not possible, and using the wrong context can be really off-putting for some students, preventing them from being able to do their best in the assessment.

So, while it may feel that including context is making your assessment more interesting or engaging, our advice would be to avoid context unless it is absolutely necessary in terms of why and what you want to assess.

Create assessment tasks that produce the evidence you need

Using illustrations in assessment tasks and items

Adding illustrations to assessment tasks and items is something else that may be done with the best of intentions, such as to make the assessment more interesting and engaging. But adding illustrations can cause similar problems to those created by adding contexts, and sometimes more! Especially since you are likely to have to use an illustration that has not been explicitly designed for your assessment, your illustration might be intended to be helpful but is quite likely to add difficulty or cause confusion. For example, if your illustration is just that – something to make the page look prettier and not something for the student to use in their answer – research has shown us that many students will waste some time trying to work out the significance of the illustration and whether and how they have to use it. Some students will go out of their way to use it, and the illustration will actually lead them to respond incorrectly to the item.

Even when you intend the student to use the illustration, it is surprisingly easy for aspects of an illustration to contradict, or appear to contradict, the wording of an item and make the student doubt their understanding. Illustrations often have irrelevant details that distract or mislead students. A picture also might be upsetting or offensive in some way. The image of a 'typical family' could be upsetting to a student that is not part of such a family (including many students that have experienced care homes or similar) or one that is recently bereaved; images of some animals can be offensive to students of certain religions; stereotypical roles could cause an emotional reaction in many students! Illustrations are also directly discriminatory to students with impaired vision, and as we saw in Chapter 2, it is best to start by trying to design your assessment to be inclusive and accessible for *all* students. The best thing is to avoid illustrations as far as possible. Simple and straightforward assessment is best.

> Clear communication is difficult, and there are many ways in which it can be disrupted. Only use context and illustration when necessary and then with great care.

Classroom Assessment for Teachers

Including optional tasks or items in your assessment

You might think that allowing students to choose from amongst different options in an assessment gives them a better chance to show what they know and can do. One problem with this can be that optional items can make an assessment too easy, allowing students to try to guess or predict what is going to come up, and prepare to be assessed on only part of the course. Take a look at any student forum on social media just before national or state exam time, and you will see young people 'question spotting', that is, coming up with lots of reasons why they are only going to study one part of the course. It's optional items that make this possible.

In other ways, optional tasks or items can make the assessment harder for some students! It can make an assessment complex for you to mark and for your students to understand. This isn't just about the practicality of the assessment. We also need to make sure that we're not assessing a student's ability to follow a complex set of instructions. If we are, we are assessing reading skills, working memory and problem-solving skills – not the history, geography or other topic that we are trying to assess. Our assessment becomes less valid.

Making the choice can itself be a real challenge. Many students make the wrong choice. It is often the already disadvantaged students who make poor choices of this kind. Good students tend to make good choices from among optional items, and poor students tend to make poorer choices. So your optional items may not make your assessment more valid, reliable and fair, they may well make it less so by helping the good students to do even better and preventing the poorer students from being able to best show what they know and can do.

> Optional tasks or items can make assessment less valid, reliable and fair. Use only with care!

Create assessment tasks that produce the evidence you need

Including scaffolding or stages in your assessment task or items

Designing an assessment task or item to be done in stages is often supportive for students. Scaffolding is often part of the learning process – you don't expect students to know everything straight away – and it can be helpful to use it in assessment, too. However, like other details of assessment, you need to take care when doing so. Scaffolding or breaking up an assessment task or item can make it more straightforward, but it can, if done badly, make it too easy. An earlier part of the item or task can all-too-easily give away (implicitly or even explicitly) the answer to a later part. For example, if the question 'What do plants need to grow?' is followed by the question 'Why do plants need water to grow?', then the second question has given away the answer to the first!

Having said care needs to be taken, scaffolded or staged tasks or items can be really useful and helpful for both the teacher and the student. They allow you to assess different aspects of a topic or a set of related skills in a way that is efficient. For example, where you want to obtain evidence of knowledge, critical thinking skills and the ability to evaluate sources (as you might in many social science or humanities assessments), you might use an essay-type item. If you also want evidence that the student can find out information for themselves, you might include a project in your assessment. Both of these can include some 'scaffolding' to help students to know what is expected of them and to structure their work in line with this. Even at higher levels of learning, scaffolding can be useful to make your requirements clear. For example, you might want to let the student know how many marks will be assigned to each separate requirement of a project or essay-type item to help them plan how much work to put into each part of their response.

> Scaffolding in assessment can help to make clearer to students what they need to do.

Care also needs to be taken that poor performance on one stage of the task or item doesn't make it harder for the student to do well in a later stage. For example, if an arithmetical error in an earlier section is carried through to a later section, but the student shows that they know how to do the later calculation, then it would be unfair not to award them at least some marks for knowing how to solve the problem, even if they haven't actually solved it correctly. Going back to the need to make sure that everyone knows exactly what it is that they have to do in an assessment, it is important to let students know that the task or item will be marked in this way. Otherwise, you run the risk that a student who knows that they answered one part of a task or item badly feels intimidated, or even paralysed, by the next part. If this feeling continues for the rest of the assessment, it can also affect how well they do on later parts, too, meaning that a relatively small error can have a very big effect on an assessment outcome.

Avoiding assessment drift

In this chapter, we have focussed on some of the decisions you will have to make when you are devising assessment tasks or items for your students. We have described different kinds of tasks and items designed to elicit different kinds of evidence for assessment. We have highlighted important considerations for valid assessment: communication, command verbs, contexts, illustrations, optional items and scaffolding. In all of this, what we have been trying to show is the importance of having an absolutely clear line of sight from what you want to assess and for what purpose, to every aspect of an assessment – from assessment methods and conditions to instructions for students and, as we will consider further in the next chapter, instructions for assessors. Alignment is the word often given to this. Any lack of alignment risks reducing validity, reliability or fairness, and lack of alignment can also introduce complications and mismatches that affect practical aspects of your assessment, too. To avoid this, you need to keep checking back to the focus of assessment and make sure the evidence being gathered or generated is exactly and only what is needed.

Create assessment tasks that produce the evidence you need

Good assessment requires alignment from what you want to assess and for what purpose, to how relevant and adequate evidence is obtained and judged and how the outcomes of that assessment are used. We must beware of assessment drift. That means when assessment begins to drift away from that clear line of sight, and your alignment begins to wobble! The wrong choice of method, task or item can result in lack of alignment, but one common cause of assessment drift can be the temptation to try to make an assessment 'interesting' or 'engaging'. Adding embellishment without good reason causes the kinds of problems we described earlier in the chapter. Any assessment should focus sharply on what is being assessed, and only that. Anything else will make your assessment less valid and will risk reducing its reliability, fairness and practicality.

> Beware assessment drift because it will undermine the validity of your assessment.

Assessment context and conditions of assessment

Assessment context

When devising good assessment, consider the context in which it will take place. Our focus in this book is on classroom assessment, but the classrooms we are thinking of can be located in many places: the workplace, the community, on a mountain, in a swimming pool, or even (at least partially) in the student's own home. You can see that the assessment you might devise for each of these classrooms could vary greatly.

> Consider the context for assessment and devise your assessment accordingly.

Classroom Assessment for Teachers

Wherever it is, classroom assessment might involve almost continuous judging of evidence gathered during the course of learning. It might include an important summative assessment that happens only once a year. Or it might be anything in between. If your assessment is one that is less frequent and with more significant consequences, you will want to be especially careful to ensure that the conditions in which it is carried out contribute to assessment validity, reliability and fairness.

Conditions of assessment

For example, is it right to allow students to access books or other resources during assessment? Should they have a limited time in which to complete the assessment? Should they work alone or can (and should) they work with others? Can they be supported during the assessment? Can they undertake any part of the assessment outside the classroom? Should there be an upper or lower limit to the number of words a student should produce? Such decisions should be made on the basis of what you really want to assess.

If you need evidence that students have memorised some knowledge, then it would *not* be appropriate to let them look up that knowledge in a book during assessment. If you want to know that they can find knowledge and then apply it, then it would be absolutely right to give them the resources they need to do that.

Is time pressure really important to the skills being assessed? If you are looking for evidence of knowledge, does it matter whether I can produce my evidence in a short period of time? Or is pressure to respond to the task quickly an irrelevance, making the assessment invalid and unfair? On the other hand, sometimes it is important to be able to work quickly. It would be appropriate in the assessment of barista skills or emergency medicine! If students really need to show that they can do something quickly, then a timed assessment would be appropriate. If not, the time available for an assessment should be sufficiently generous that no undue time pressure is applied. Time

Create assessment tasks that produce the evidence you need

limits are often introduced for practical reasons – and practicality is certainly important provided it does not add to the challenge of an assessment unnecessarily.

If assessment is of a process and students can't complete it without some feedback during that process, then allowing some level of support can be justified. But how much? And how do you ensure that everyone gets the same amount of support?

The decision about whether students are allowed to complete some part of an assessment outside the classroom must be thought through very carefully. On the one hand, an extended assessment like a project of some kind might require more time for research or development of ideas than is available in class time. On the other hand, being able to do some part of an assessment at home might be unfair to students who have less space, time or resources than others.

If you want to know what the student knows and can do alone, then they should be required to work alone during assessment, and it would be reasonable to supervise them to make sure that is what happens. If you want to know that the student can work with others, then the assessment must be designed to allow that to happen instead.

A word limit might force students to be more succinct and that can be a challenge. If this is one of the skills you want to assess, then restricting the word limit is appropriate. If it's not a focus for assessment, then don't, although you might want to give some guidance on how many words you expect for reasons of practicality. It's a fine balance but an important one to seek if you want your assessment to be focused on what's important.

Exactly how the assessment is to be carried out is an important *part of* the assessment. Decisions about the conditions under which assessment is to be carried out contribute in important ways to its validity.

Classroom Assessment for Teachers

They need to be thought through just as carefully as any other part of the assessment.

> Assessment conditions are an important part of assessment and should contribute to assessment validity.

Efficiency in assessment

For ethical reasons, it is important that assessment is efficient. Generating much more evidence than you need would, therefore, be unethical. Assessment should provide just enough of the right kind of evidence – no more and no less.

> Assessment that is both ethical and valid should provide just enough of the right kind of evidence.

While each assessment should be sharply focused on generating particular kinds of evidence, it is possible to create an assessment that generates evidence for more than one kind of knowledge or skill. Getting as much evidence as possible out of a single assessment can be a good and ethical approach.

On the other hand, trying to get too much out of an assessment can cause problems. It may make the assessment take so long to do that

Create assessment tasks that produce the evidence you need

the student gets tired. It may be so complicated to follow that the student gets confused. In such cases, it may be better for the student to undertake a number of smaller assessments than a single big, complicated one.

> **Practical Step 5:**
> *Make sure any assessment task can provide you with the right kind and the right amount of evidence for assessment, in the right conditions, as directly and efficiently as possible, and communicate very clearly to students what they need to do.*

Summary

In this chapter, we introduced the idea of 'a test worth teaching to' and focused on how to devise such an assessment task. As with any assessment, we want to generate enough of the right kind of evidence for assessment. That means not only the chosen method but also the task or assessment item are able to generate the right kind of evidence as directly and efficiently as possible. That task or item must help the student to produce the required evidence for assessment and in the right amount. To do this, clear communication is essential. There are recognised risks to such communication associated with certain features of assessment tasks, such as contexts and illustrations. Optionality can seem helpful but can also cause problems for assessment quality. Similarly, scaffolding can be useful but must be used with care. The most important thing for valid assessment is to ensure alignment of all decisions with the purpose and focus of your assessment and to communicate clearly to students what it is they need to do. Assessment context is an important consideration, and conditions of assessment are very relevant to assessment validity. Finally, for ethical reasons, the efficiency of any assessment task is also important.

9 Judging evidence for assessment

This chapter is all about

- The importance of alignment in all parts of assessment, including the judging of evidence
- Why the instructions for judging evidence for assessment should be devised at the same time as any assessment item or task and before intended learning has begun
- Different approaches to judging evidence, including marking and grading
- The importance of clear communication with assessors and students
- The quality assurance of assessment

Just as important for high-quality assessment as the clarity of instructions to students, the instructions that the assessor (you – or others) will use for judging the evidence the student produces are critical. Instructions for students and instructions for assessors cannot be separated. They should be written at the same time, and there should be complete alignment between them and with the chosen purpose and focus of the assessment.

The importance of alignment

The assessment task for the student and the instructions on judging the student's assessment evidence *must* be created together, and both

Judging evidence for assessment

should be closely aligned with the focus of your assessment (what you are assessing and what evidence of that will look like) and the purpose of your assessment (why you are assessing and what the outcomes of assessment will be used for). This applies to all methods of assessment – from a written exam to a dance performance.

Good assessment comes from keeping a focus on . . .

- what students are expected to know and be able to do, which tells you . . .
- what evidence for assessment you need *and* . . .
- how that evidence should be judged

> Assessment *is* the way that evidence for assessment is generated or gathered **and** the way that evidence is judged.

Creating your instructions for judging evidence at the same time as creating your instructions for students should help you to develop an assessment that is fit for purpose, as you will have that purpose in mind as you decide what sort of evidence you are looking for as well as how you will judge that evidence. You may find it helpful to ask yourself:

- What do I want students to show me that they know or can do?
- How do I think they will show me this? What evidence will allow me to judge that they have acquired that knowledge or those skills?
- How will I arrive at consistent judgements about the evidence that my students produce?

It may sound obvious, but it can be quite easy to decide on an assessment method, task or item because it seems like an interesting idea, is what you experienced when you were a student or is what a colleague suggests. But if you do this without thinking through whether it is actually the best way to obtain the kind of evidence you are looking for, your assessment might fall down at the first hurdle. If you start by asking yourself those three questions provided, then you are, in effect, starting by thinking, 'What's the answer I am looking for?' Sounds silly, but this will put you in a better place to answer the question, 'So how do I give my students the best chance to show me that they know or can do that?' and to be sure that you are rewarding exactly the knowledge and skills you need evidence of and not irrelevant qualities, such as attractive presentation, tidiness or speed.

> To make sure your assessment will provide exactly the evidence you need, you might find it useful to start by thinking about how you will judge that evidence.

That is why some have argued that to make sure that your assessment task or item will generate exactly the evidence you need, begin with the answers! Start with the evidence you're looking for, think about how you will reward that evidence, and then create your tasks or items to make it as easy as possible for students to produce exactly that evidence:

1. Start with exactly what you want your student to be able to show they know or can do and how that is to be valued
2. Create your task or items in a way that will most clearly and directly elicit that evidence

If you first identify clearly what you're looking for and want to reward, then you can more easily determine the questions or instructions that will direct the student to produce exactly that! You can also be clearer and more confident about what evidence for assessment you might look out for during learning.

Judging evidence for assessment

This approach also makes perfect sense if you intend to gather naturally occurring evidence rather than using an assessment task to generate it. In this case, your job is to think carefully about the kinds and amounts of evidence you need and how that will be valued, and then to look out for it as it occurs naturally in your classroom.

Instructions to self!

Clear instructions for judging evidence will help different assessors to assess consistently, and that is important for assessment reliability. But it is also important if you are developing and using your own assessments with your own students. Setting down in writing how you intend to mark or judge your evidence for assessment will help you to think carefully about what is important. It will help you to make consistent assessment decisions, rewarding responses in the same way each time you judge each student's evidence. It can provide you with a handy reminder of what you're looking for and remind you that your judgement is (usually) not about comparing one student's evidence to another's. It will also help you to judge more objectively and to minimise the unconscious biases to which we are all prone.

Creating clear instructions for judging or marking evidence for assessment can also help you to check whether the evidence you're looking for, and how you plan to reward it, is exactly right for what and why you are assessing. Clear and clean alignment between the purpose and focus of your assessment, the way you plan to gather or generate the evidence and how you will reward that evidence is essential for good assessment.

> For valid assessment, there should be a clear line of sight from purpose and focus of assessment, through how evidence for assessment is gathered or generated, to how that evidence is judged.

Classroom Assessment for Teachers

Students should know how their evidence will be judged

In order to be fair to all students, you should make sure that they are clear about what they need to do to be successful in assessment. This means they should know how they will be assessed and how their evidence for assessment will be judged, whether that evidence is gathered naturally in the course of learning or generated using an assessment task. This information will help them during their preparation as well as during the assessment. It will help them to manage their response to assessment, for example, by planning how much time to spend on each aspect of it. So, when you are setting out to gather or generate evidence for assessment, your instructions (perhaps to yourself) on how to judge that evidence should be in place before the assessment takes place.

> For valid assessment, students should be clear about what evidence you're looking for and also how that evidence will be judged.

Approaches to marking or judging evidence for assessment

In previous chapters, we saw that your choice of assessment tasks and items should make it easy for your students to show you the kind of evidence for assessment you're looking for.

If you want to know whether a student knows something, or can do something, or not, then your choice of item type will suit that kind of evidence for assessment, and your instructions for marking or judging that evidence will be easy!

On the other hand, if you expect your students to provide evidence for assessment that demonstrates different amounts of knowledge or

Judging evidence for assessment

skills, then your task or item will need to be of a type that allows that evidence to be provided, and your instructions for marking or judging that evidence will need to allow for such a range of student responses. When you are marking or judging assessment evidence of this sort, there will be no objectively correct answers for you to look for. Instead, you will need clear criteria upon which to judge the range of responses that students might produce to demonstrate the knowledge and skills that you are assessing.

Whatever kind of assessment task or item you create, the instructions for judging evidence should match precisely what students have been asked to do, and assessors should understand exactly how that evidence is to be judged. Marking instructions should be as clear and as explicit as possible. This will make assessment more efficient as well as more reliable. Any approach to making assessment judgements should minimise subjectivity and the risk of irrelevant factors being taken into account. Attractive presentation might be relevant to assessing cake decorating but completely irrelevant when assessing a portfolio of creative writing. Neatness of the product might be very important for the assessment of joinery skills. It should be not at all relevant to a poster that students have been asked to create simply as a fun way to *demonstrate their knowledge* of the solar system.

> If evidence for assessment is generated using an assessment task or item, the way it is judged should exactly match what students have been asked to do.

How you judge your students' evidence will depend not only on what you are assessing or on how you are assessing it but also on why you are assessing it. If, for example, the purpose is to differentiate between students, you may want to rank their evidence for assessment in some way and assign marks or grades accordingly. If your assessment is primarily designed for a summative purpose, then it may in any case be helpful to assign grades or similar, as handy shorthand for recording and reporting purposes. If your assessment has a formative purpose, that is, to help you and the student to understand what they need to do in their next learning steps, then you will want the judgement of evidence to result in some kind of commentary on strengths and weaknesses. We say more about the different forms that assessment outcomes might take in Chapter 10.

> For valid assessment, the approach to judging evidence should be appropriate to your assessment purpose.

Why you are carrying out the assessment will be your first consideration as you begin to create your instructions for judging evidence for assessment. As we saw in Chapter 4, a clear purpose that is aligned with your intended learning outcomes, if you use them, is the starting point for good assessment. That applies to the marking or judging stage of assessment as much as to any other stage. Let's think about that in a bit more detail. Table 9.1 shows how approaches to marking or judging of evidence relate to different kinds of assessment purpose.

Some kinds of assessment are much less interested in gradations of student performance than in whether a specified level of competence has been demonstrated. Such assessments have criteria against which evidence is intended to be judged simply as met (for example, a 'pass') or not met. It may be a requirement that all parts of an assessment are passed or only some that might or might not be specified. Those decisions will depend on the purpose and focus of the assessment. For example, in the case of assessments of professional competence for doctors, driving instructors, electricians and so on, decisions on whether professional standards have been reached

Judging evidence for assessment

Table 9.1 How instructions for judging evidence for assessment relate to assessment purpose

Why are you assessing your students?	What sort of marking or judging instructions will you need?
Your purpose is formative. You want to focus on identifying next steps in learning.	The way you mark or judge evidence for assessment will be aimed at helping you to identify next steps in learning. It is likely to take the form of a commentary that identifies strengths and areas for improvement. Instructions should provide broad guidance for the assessor.
Your purpose is summative and is aimed at checking completion of a topic or unit. You simply want to confirm course or topic completion or that your students have acquired an acceptable level of competence.	The marking or judging instructions will focus on identifying a level of performance that can be judged as competent, a pass or satisfactory completion. This will also allow you to judge which students are not yet competent, have not passed or have not yet satisfactorily completed the course of learning that you are assessing.
(Although the primary purpose of this assessment is not formative, of course, the outcomes can be used for formative purposes. For example, to identify students that need some additional time or support and where those needs lie.)	

(*Continued*)

Table 9.1 (Continued)

Why are you assessing your students?	What sort of marking or judging instructions will you need?
Your purpose is summative, and you need to be able to differentiate between different levels of student achievement. Often this kind of assessment is used for reporting to others – other teachers, students and their parents or carers. The same assessment outcomes can also be used to guide next steps in learning, for example, to support decision-making by the student or others on appropriate courses of learning that are at different levels of complexity.	The marking or judging instructions will need to allow you to assign different outcomes to different students. It will likely use marks (which you may later convert to grades) or direct grading. Either of these is likely to need detailed descriptions of different levels of performance.

or not will recognise the consequences *for others* of someone passing when they should not, by comparison with the consequences for the individual of someone failing when they should have passed. The instructions for judging evidence for assessment in those cases should be designed accordingly.

Once you have thought through the implications of why you are carrying out your assessment and how you might go about judging your evidence, it will also be useful to spend a bit of time reflecting on who your students are. In Chapter 5, we noted how easy it is to give this question less attention than it deserves, but how important it is to create your assessment with particular students in mind and to ensure that no student is excluded unnecessarily. This consideration is just as

Judging evidence for assessment

important when deciding how you are going to mark or judge evidence as it is when creating your assessment tasks or items.

For example, it may or may not be relevant to include spelling or handwriting in your criteria for judging evidence for assessment. It may or may not be relevant to reward presentation, or speed, or length or succinctness. Each of these things might be wholly relevant to what you are assessing, but if it is not, then that could mean students being judged unfairly or even being prevented altogether from showing what they know and can do. When deciding on how you are going to judge or mark your students' evidence, it is important to take time to think about the whole group of students you are assessing and how you can ensure that your assessment is as fair and inclusive as possible for the range of individuals within that group.

> Judging of evidence should be tightly aligned with the focus of your assessment and reward only what is relevant to that.

And, of course, when you are deciding how you are going to judge your students' evidence, what you are assessing and how you are assessing it will be key. An assessment of a body of knowledge, whether that uses oral questioning or a written test, naturally lends itself to using marks for each item. Even if each assessment item is simply right or wrong, it may be useful to assign marks to each item so that you can more easily provide an overall outcome for the assessment. You will want to ensure that you mark this evidence consistently by developing instructions that lay out key principles, broad guidance for yourself and other markers as well as detailed instructions on what responses should be rewarded with marks and, sometimes, which responses should not be accepted. These instructions should go into enough detail to remind you – and make it clear to others using your assessment – how many marks should be awarded for each response. This will be especially important where partial responses may be awarded a share of an overall number of marks. Good marking instructions should make clear the total marks available for the assessment, how many for each part of the assessment and for each item and how each of those marks should be awarded.

> The marking instructions for good assessment should make clear to assessors how marks are to be awarded and for what.

Allocating marks to different parts of an assessment

Thinking about how many marks might be available for different parts of an assessment makes us consider the relative importance of what is being assessed. Valid assessment might need a minimum standard to be met in all its parts, for example, if the assessment is of professional competence. If not, you might want to assign greater importance to one part of an assessment than another, and one simple way to do that is to allow more marks for one part than another. You would want to be able to justify that decision on the basis of assessment validity. For example, knowledge about flour types may be less important than the skill to combine flour with other ingredients to make an excellent cake! The skills required to put up a shelf may be less important than strict adherence to health and safety practices. The ability to draw a neat graph may be less important than the knowledge and skills required to interpret complex graphical data. This is all about weightings within an assessment.

When you are making decisions of this kind, you should be able to justify your approach to marking, weighting and grading in ways that relate to the validity of your assessment. For example, you may feel that one part of an assessment should carry more weight than another

Judging evidence for assessment

because it is assessing a longer period of learning. It might be assessing learning that you feel is more important, such as safe practices, in which a 'pass' might be required while weaknesses in other parts of an assessment might be tolerated. How many marks of the total available should constitute a 'pass'? Can a good performance on one part of an assessment compensate for a poor performance on another? Your answer to every one of these questions will have an impact on the validity of your assessment.

> Every decision about how evidence will be rewarded will have an impact on the validity of your assessment.

Turning marks into grades

If you need grades for recording or reporting purposes, it may be appropriate and possible to grade a student's evidence directly. For example, in skills-based assessments, you may be able to grade a performance by comparing it to a series of grade-related criteria. Alternatively, you might want or need to start with marking an assessment and converting those marks into a single grade or sometimes a few grades. This is the kind of process used by many organisations that provide assessment for national qualifications or other kinds of standardised assessments. In this process, the marks on different parts of an assessment are translated into grades representing different levels of performance on it, which are intended to convey meaning to the users of the assessment outcomes. Very careful thought must be given to what each grade is intended to mean, and the way in which marks are turned into grades should ensure that it does mean just that. Without such careful thought, the validity of the assessment can be undermined.

> The way in which marks are turned into grades – whether that is a 'pass' or 'fail', an 'A', 'B' or 'C' – will contribute to assessment validity or can undermine it.

The critical importance of communication

However you decide your evidence for assessment is to be judged – by allocating marks for correct responses, for example, or by judging against broader criteria – it is critical for valid assessment to communicate that very clearly and unambiguously to assessors. Assessment reliability is heavily dependent upon assessors making consistent judgements. That means minimising the requirement or scope for assessors to make subjective judgements, even when assessment items or tasks are likely to elicit a range of responses from students. It should not be up to assessors to decide while judging evidence what is important and what is not, what kind of student response is deserving of marks and what is not. Where there is no objectively 'correct' response, the assessor must be given clear guidelines to follow so that different assessors can and should judge a piece of evidence in the same way as far as that is possible. While that can never be guaranteed, providing assessors with very clear and unambiguous instructions is an important starting point upon which quality assurance, including moderation processes, can build.

> For assessment reliability and validity, instructions for judging evidence for assessment should be communicated very clearly and unambiguously to those who will use them.

Quality assurance

We are all familiar with the idea of quality assurance. We expect it to be carefully applied during the making, selecting, storing or transporting of the products we use: our cars, our children's toys, our tins of beans and our bags of apples. We expect it to be routinely applied when the services we need or want are being provided: telecoms, electricity, public transport, retail and restaurant experiences, to name just a very few. Quality assurance is an important consideration for everyone because failure to provide a quality product or experience will have negative consequences for the provider of these goods and services as well as for us. Some kinds of educational assessment can also have very significant consequences for the student. For that reason, and especially for those kinds of assessment, quality assurance is essential. It is also useful to quality assure any assessment activity.

For assessment that has significant consequences for the student or others, quality assurance may be provided by an external organisation, such as an education authority, a school group or an organisation providing assessments set statewide or nationally. In these instances, there may be clear requirements of any internal quality assurance when marking is done in schools.

If you are creating assessments for a number of teachers to use, you may also want to consider other steps to ensure your instructions are applied consistently. Within schools, better assessment can be quality assured through activities like professional dialogue about assessments, meetings with colleagues from the same or other schools to discuss student responses to a particular assessment, or arrangements to cross-mark all or a selection of each other's marking. All of these activities can contribute to better assessment and increased expertise for you as teachers. This may be formalised in documented moderation practices, or it can be much less formal but no less valuable for teachers.

Classroom Assessment for Teachers

> *Practical Step 6:*
> *Whether evidence for assessment is gathered during learning or generated using an assessment task, make sure that instructions for judging it are aligned with purpose and focus, match what students are asked to do and are communicated clearly to assessors and shared with students.*

Summary

In this chapter, we explained the importance of keeping in mind the purpose and focus of your assessment as you determine how evidence for assessment should be judged. The way in which a student's evidence is rewarded should also be absolutely aligned with what you have asked students to do to produce that evidence. Instructions for judging evidence for assessment should be written at the same time as the task for students. It has even been argued that decisions on how to reward evidence for assessment should be made *before* the assessment task is created so the task can be focused on producing exactly that evidence. If evidence for assessment is being gathered during learning, then it will be helpful to be clear in advance about what evidence will be sought and how that will be valued. The chapter covered different approaches to judging evidence for assessment according to the purpose of assessment, ideas about weightings in assessment, how marks can be turned into grades and how these can impact upon assessment validity. Finally, we explained the importance for assessment quality of communicating clearly how evidence for assessment is to be judged and why quality assurance can make an important and, sometimes, essential contribution to the quality of assessment.

10 Making good use of the outcomes of assessment

This chapter is all about

- How forms of assessment outcomes should relate to purpose and uses
- Important considerations when sharing assessment outcomes with students and others

The end of an assessment process is not the assessment outcomes, it is the use to which those outcomes are put.

Using assessment outcomes according to assessment purpose

In earlier chapters, we described two main purposes that a teacher might have for devising educational assessment, and associated uses for the resulting assessment outcomes – summative and formative. We also made clear that any assessment has the potential to serve both of those purposes although better assessment is likely to result when you have one or other purpose clearly in mind while creating it. However, what makes an assessment distinctly formative or summative is the use that is made of its outcomes.

> What makes any assessment either formative or summative is the use to which assessment outcomes are put.

Choosing when and how best to communicate assessment outcomes can have a powerful impact on engagement and learning – and you want to ensure that this impact is positive. There is no point in the teacher learning important things about the student if those cannot be used to engage the student in their own learning journey.

Assessment outcomes can open doors for students – to opportunities for further learning or for work. In this case, assessment outcomes are often shared not only with students but also with others who are gatekeepers to those opportunities, from university admissions staff to teachers in the next academic year. Parents and carers, too, will often have access to assessment outcomes. For assessment outcomes to be used appropriately, it is important for those receiving them to understand clearly what they mean.

> For ethical assessment, those using assessment outcomes should understand what those outcomes can and can't tell us.

Forms of assessment outcomes

We have already argued that if educational assessment is to be undertaken at all, it should have a clear purpose. The ways in which assessment outcomes are used should relate to that purpose, and the form that assessment outcomes take should be designed to allow them to be used in that way.

Making good use of the outcomes of assessment

> Assessment outcomes should be fit for the assessment purpose and used in that way.

Before we consider in any detail when and how you will want to share assessment outcomes, it is useful to say a little more about the forms that assessment outcomes might take. There are advantages and disadvantages to each of these typical approaches. Most educational assessment will use one or the other, but some will use both.

We can think of assessment outcomes taking two main forms. One of these, and the most valuable for student learning, is some kind of commentary on the strengths and weaknesses the student has demonstrated in evidence for assessment whether that is provided in the course of learning or in response to an assessment task. The other common form is the use of words or symbols that represent a summary of achievement. These could be marks or grades, or statements such as 'pass', 'fail', 'merit', 'distinction'. Assessment for summative purposes uses this kind of shorthand to communicate assessment outcomes not only to students but also to parents, carers and others who don't know and may not need to know the detail of what has or has not been learned.

- **Commentary focused on strengths and weaknesses**
  Verbal or written phrases or sentences – sometimes chosen from a pre-defined menu. This approach to reporting assessment outcomes is designed to give information about strengths and weaknesses that can be used to alter approaches to teaching or learning.
- **Summary and symbolic representations of overall performance**
  These provide an indication of overall performance in part or all of an assessment. They may be determined by performance relative to expected standards (usually explicitly described) or relative to the performances of other students in a group or in a wider population. When you are devising your own assessment, it may be better that

any symbolic representation of performance relates to expected standards and not to the performance of other students. While the latter might be rewarding for some students, it is likely to be damaging to learning and to wellbeing for others.

- Marks – numerical values which can be raw or scaled (for example, given as a % even though the original assessment was not marked out of 100). They can be given for an entire assessment or presented as a profile of marks for different parts of an assessment.
- Grades – often a letter value (for example, 'A' to 'F') representing the overall performance on an assessment. These grades can be derived from marks or can be awarded directly.
- Verbal categories such as 'pass', 'competent', 'distinction'. These can be derived from marks or can be awarded directly.

If you are using a commercial or other externally provided assessment, you may find that it provides you with outcomes in only one of these forms although some may offer you the option to select from or use two or more of them. Usually, there will be an explanation of what the assessment outcomes mean. Such an explanation should be written in a way that makes it easy for you to understand *and* for you to explain to your students.

If you have the option to select the form of the assessment outcome, and always if you are developing and using your own assessments, you should spend some time thinking about the purpose or purposes (such as recording for your own records and/or for reporting to others) to which the assessment outcomes are to be put, especially if these will be shared with students.

Assessment outcomes fit for assessment purposes

Chapter 4 described three main purposes for assessment in a classroom context: formative, summative and diagnostic. The outcomes for

Making good use of the outcomes of assessment

each of these purposes should be designed to best suit that purpose. The ways in which they are communicated should in every case be designed to maximise the positive benefits and minimise any negative effects on your students.

> For ethical assessment, when communicating assessment outcomes the priority should be to maximise benefits and minimise harms.

Using assessment outcomes for formative purposes

One key idea that most assessment for learning experts agree on is that outcomes that provide too high level a summary – too little detail – can be unhelpful. Put baldly, sharing marks or grades can get in the way of learning rather than support it. If you are assessing for formative purposes, the outcomes that you will be sharing should take the form of comments about the student's evidence for assessment.

> For formative purposes, assessment outcomes should take the form of comments rather than marks or grades.

When you are using assessment outcomes for formative purposes, you will want to make it clear to students from the start what it is that they will be learning. You can then use assessment outcomes to identify and share strengths and weaknesses and what they need to do next to progress in their learning.

Your feedback should always be aimed at engaging the students in their own learning and should provide them with information that helps them to plan their next steps. Your comments to students should note what was done well, then identify specific areas for improvement and what to do to make those improvements, while also communicating that progress is in the hands of the student, supported by you. Your comments should be specific in identifying qualities of the individual student's work, in objective terms, and not in comparison with other students. You might liken this to interview feedback: whilst it may be comforting to hear, 'You were pipped for the job by one person', that doesn't tell you what you need to do differently next time to have a better chance of getting the job! So, if you are giving feedback to students on their writing skills, you don't want to make general statements like 'Your paragraphs need work'. Instead, you need to talk about some features of their work that are good and some that could be improved. It's always about looking forward to the next steps in learning and giving students the information that they need to help them to take those steps. That is why this sort of commentary is sometimes called 'feed-forward' rather than 'feedback'.

> Formative feedback should provide students with information that helps them to learn, in a way that engages them in that learning.

To ensure that your feedback is effective, there is evidence that it is best delivered through a discussion between the teacher and the student. If comments or feedback have to be provided in writing, students might be encouraged to reflect on these and to discuss them with their peers to help engage students in their own assessment and future learning. If a group of students has completed the same assessment, it can be useful to share feedback with a group of students at the same time or to ask students to share outcomes with each other: encouraging dialogue between students has been

Making good use of the outcomes of assessment

found to be a very useful tool in helping students to understand their own learning processes and take more active control of them. It makes sense to do this as soon as possible after the assessment has taken place.

The impacts of assessment outcomes on students can be cognitive and that is often the first thing we think about. But what has at least as important an impact on learning is how sharing those outcomes makes students *feel*. That can in turn depend upon how engaged the student is and how supported, how motivated and how resilient. It can be influenced by the cultural and social context of your classroom and beyond. It is, therefore, important to consider what kind of feedback to provide to each student that will have a positive impact on learning and minimise any risk of negative impacts. Those benefits and harms are strongly linked to the ways in which the outcomes of assessment are communicated and used. No matter how well designed an assessment, if the outcomes are used inappropriately then damage to learning and learners can ensue.

> Sharing assessment outcomes can have important impacts on how students feel as well as how they think, and learning can be affected by both.

It is not always necessary to communicate the outcomes of assessment to students: for example, when you are making a series of micro-assessments as a lesson progresses, you may just need to adjust your next teaching action. In the case of more formal assessments, if the outcomes are not good, there is a risk that sharing them could undermine student confidence and engagement. However, the United Nations Convention on the Rights of the Child (UNCRC) requires that students have agency in their learning, and research tell us that such agency leads to better learning.

Classroom Assessment for Teachers

Using assessment outcomes for summative purposes

It is also in the realm of assessment for summative purposes that educational and assessment professionals should take great care about how to use assessment outcomes, especially when those outcomes take the form of a single mark or grade. The purpose of these is to communicate what has been learned in a way that can be understood by those not familiar with the content of the course of learning. For this purpose, they are ideal. They can also provide useful information to the teacher and the student.

> The outcomes of assessment for summative purposes are intended to be meaningful shorthand for those not familiar with the course of learning, mainly useful for recording or reporting.

Assessment outcomes summarised as grades, numbers or phrases – 'good', 'excellent', etc – are shorthand descriptions of different levels of performance. When these are based on criteria that are clear to the student, they can help students to know where they are on their learning journey and are more helpful if they are also accompanied by comments designed to guide future learning.

Too much focus on grades can lead to students taking a very transactional approach to what they learn. They may focus on trying to get 'the biggest bang for their buck' in learning time: the greatest potential increase in marks or grades for the least possible effort. This may include focussing on rote learning or memorisation, unwillingness to engage with more complex and difficult learning scenarios to which there may be no 'correct' answer and not wanting to learn anything that isn't 'in the test'. They may take fewer risks in their learning and be less willing to employ creativity and originality. In short, an overfocus on grades can result in superficial rather than deep learning.

Making good use of the outcomes of assessment

If you want the outcomes of summative assessment to also have a positive impact on learning, you may want to withhold any mark or grade until after you have had a chance to share comments and after the student has had a chance to assimilate these. Like any feedback, you will want to do this as quickly as possible after the assessment has taken place so that even if you are moving on from the topic or area of learning, the students will remember their learning activities and have maximum chances of reflecting on what they can learn from their assessment outcomes.

Using assessment outcomes for diagnostic purposes

If you have used an assessment designed for diagnostic purposes, it should inform you, as the teacher, about the starting point for a student's learning or what specific learning difficulties a student may be experiencing. You can use that information to plan the most effective learning interventions or the most suitable course of learning. As we noted in Chapter 4, when you are assessing for diagnostic purposes, you are likely to be using an assessment devised by others. That assessment should provide you with advice on the form that outcomes will take, what they mean and how you should act on those outcomes. Your job is to do this with care and thought for the impact on the student, so you can engage them in any supportive intervention that follows.

Communicating assessment outcomes beyond the classroom

Even if you devise and use most of your assessments for formative purposes, you will sometimes have to create and use them for summative purposes in order to report outcomes to people who are not part of your daily classroom interactions. Grades are useful, for example, to provide reports to parents or to provide summaries of your students' achievements when they are ready to move on to another educational establishment or into work.

Classroom Assessment for Teachers

In these instances, whilst your assessment outcomes may include a narrative element (such as a series of 'Can do' statements that relate to a defined curriculum), the assessment outcome is much more likely to take the form of marks or grades. These may be reported individually for different subjects or parts of the course of learning or aggregated into an overall score or grade point average. If you have some choice over this, your aim should be to provide as much useable information as possible. However, often the form of such assessment outcomes is dictated by external organisations. In some instances, you will want to make sure that you have discussed the assessment outcomes with your students before reporting it to others. In other instances, particularly for high-stakes external assessments, you may not know the assessment outcomes before your students do, and your role will be to ensure that you are available to them to interpret their results and think objectively about what it means for their next stage of learning or life.

For an assessment to be valid, the assessment outcomes must be meaningful. They must be telling us what we need to know. In the case of summative assessment, we should be reasonably confident that a student with an 'A' grade is likely to know and be able to do a bit more than one with a 'B' grade and much more than one with an 'E' grade. The same is true for all other ways of typically reporting the outcomes of summative assessment. Most parts of society take this on trust, but as a teacher, you may wish to think about this a little more deeply, not only for your own practice but for understanding any assessments taken by your students that others have produced.

> For assessment to be valid, the outcomes it produces must be meaningful to those who will use them.

Depending on the education system and stage in which you are working, there may be a culture of using marks to signal assessment outcomes

Making good use of the outcomes of assessment

or of using summary grades. There may also be school, regional, or national policies that you are required to follow. In each case, you may find it valuable to familiarise yourself with how the marks and grades are arrived at, for example, how marks are awarded, how they are combined and how that is transformed into a final outcome that can be reported. You will find it useful to be aware of how assessment outcomes are calculated in your system so that you can be clear about what inferences can and cannot be made from them. It may be that your system is one in which richer information accompanies grades to help you, parents and others to understand what the grades do or don't mean. This additional information might provide some context about the results or some details about how the final grade was derived. With or without this, if you have as much information as possible, you can use your understanding to better prepare your students for assessment and for the outcomes of such assessment.

> Using assessment outcomes well requires knowledge about what those assessment outcomes really mean.

Whatever approach to devising assessment outcomes you may have chosen or may encounter, you should aim to have a clear understanding of what assessment outcomes really *mean*. That knowledge will allow you to communicate those assessment outcomes clearly to students, colleagues, parents and carers in ways that will fulfil the purpose of the assessment.

> **Practical Step 7:**
> **Present and use assessment outcomes for the purpose for which they were intended and in ways that maximise positive impacts on students and minimize negative ones.**

Classroom Assessment for Teachers

Summary

This chapter was all about how assessment outcomes can best be used. We described the different forms of assessment outcomes and explained their relationship to assessment purposes. We outlined the ways in which assessment outcomes can be used for formative and for summative purposes to maximise benefits and minimise harms to learning and student wellbeing. Finally, we noted the importance of having a clear understanding of the meaning of assessment outcomes in order to communicate and use these appropriately. That is what makes any assessment worthwhile.

Overview of the principles of assessment and practical steps for putting these into practice

We all measure, assess and make judgements in everyday life that are valuable or even essential for giving us information we can depend upon and can use to guide our actions. In Chapters 1 to 3 of this book, we describe educational assessment in these terms and introduce the principles that underpin all good educational assessment and, indeed, most kinds of assessment or measurement.

Good educational assessment can give us important information about the kinds of things students know and can do and how well they know and can do them. We can use that information with confidence to make adjustments to how we teach or students learn, or we can record it and report on it so that others can use it with confidence, too.

Educational assessment is a process that involves gathering or generating evidence of what students know and can do, judging that evidence and making use of the resulting outcomes. It happens all the time in the classroom and varies according to its purpose, consequences, timing, frequency and formality. Teacher-devised classroom assessment most often has a formative purpose or a summative one. The intended consequences of educational assessment relate to its purposes, and its timing, frequency and formality are determined by them.

Classroom Assessment for Teachers

Whatever its purpose, good educational assessment must be valid, sufficiently reliable, fair and reasonably practical. Validity is the extent to which an assessment is in fact measuring what it is intended to measure. Reliability is the extent to which the outcomes of assessment are not influenced by things that are not relevant to what is meant to be assessed. Fairness is broadly the extent to which an assessment allows everyone an equitable opportunity to show what they know and can do, and practicality is the extent to which the assessment is manageable for student and teacher or assessor to undertake. These four qualities exist in degrees, interact with one another and determine an assessment's quality and fitness for purpose.

Whatever its intended purpose, good educational assessment will be devised and its outcomes should be used with care to maximise its benefits and minimise any risk of harms. The principles of validity, reliability, fairness and practicality, and of maximising benefits and minimising risks, underpin all good educational assessment. They inform every decision made when good educational assessment is being devised and its outcomes are being used.

Those decisions will be taken during a sequence of practical steps that are outlined next and explained more fully in Chapters 4 to 10 of this book. The content in all of these chapters relates to, and explains the relevance of, the principles underpinning all good educational assessment.

The sequence of practical steps is intended to ensure alignment from the beginning to the end of the process of assessment or of devising assessment: from why and what and who is being assessed, to how evidence for assessment is gathered or generated and that evidence is judged, to how outcomes of assessment are presented and how those outcomes of assessment are used.

Overview of the principles of assessment and practical steps

Chapter 4: Be clear about why you want to assess

> **Practical Step 1:**
> *Always begin the process of devising assessment by being clear about why you want to assess your students, and keep that purpose in mind.*

For ethical reasons, educational assessment should always have a clear purpose, and purpose should inform all decisions about assessment, including how the outcomes of assessment can be used. The two common purposes for teacher-devised classroom assessment are formative and summative, which relate to the uses to which assessment outcomes are put. When assessment is for formative purposes, the outcomes are used to inform next steps in teaching and learning. When assessment is for summative purposes, the outcomes are used as a summary of achievements to record and to report to others. While any assessment might be able to be used for more than one purpose, it will better achieve its purpose if it has been devised to do exactly that.

Chapter 5: Be clear about who you want to assess

> **Practical Step 2:**
> *Make sure your assessment is devised with your students in mind and is fair for all of your students, because inclusive assessment benefits everyone.*

As with devising assessment for a particular purpose, assessment devised for particular students is likely to work better than assessment that is not. Assessment should be fair and inclusive so that *all* students can show what they know and can do, which will contribute to assessment validity as well.

Chapter 6: Be clear about what you want to assess

> *Practical Step 3:*
> *Be very clear about what it is that you want to assess so that you can devise your assessment to obtain evidence of exactly that.*

Being clear about what you want to assess will tell you what kinds of evidence for assessment you are looking for, and that will inform later decisions about how best to obtain that evidence and to judge it.

Chapter 7: Choose approaches and methods to suit your purpose and the evidence for assessment you need

> *Practical Step 4:*
> *Choose assessment approaches and methods that will most directly and efficiently provide you with the kinds of evidence for assessment you need.*

Evidence for assessment can be gathered as it occurs naturally during learning, or it might need to be generated using an assessment task. Many methods of assessment can be used in either case – such as observation, portfolios, questioning. Decisions about such methods should rest on which will most directly and efficiently provide the evidence for assessment that you need and that is vital for establishing assessment validity. Get such early decisions wrong and it will not be possible to correct them later.

Overview of the principles of assessment and practical steps

Chapter 8: Create assessment tasks that help students produce the evidence for assessment you need

> ***Practical Step 5:***
> *Make sure any assessment task can provide you with the right kind and the right amount of evidence for assessment, in the right conditions, as directly and efficiently as possible, and communicate very clearly to students what they need to do.*

If you need to generate evidence for assessment using an assessment task, the key to valid assessment is making sure that your choice of task or item(s) will generate exactly the evidence for assessment you need. We describe two main categories of assessment task or item used across different assessment methods, which can be used to directly and efficiently generate different kinds and amounts of evidence for assessment. The role of the task is to communicate clearly to students what they are being asked to do, and we describe some common features of assessment that can support or undermine that and, therefore, assessment reliability and validity. We also explain why the context and conditions for assessment are important considerations for valid assessment.

Chapter 9: Judging evidence for assessment

> ***Practical Step 6:***
> *Whether evidence for assessment is gathered during learning or generated using an assessment task, make sure that instructions for judging it are aligned with purpose and focus, match what students are asked to do and are communicated clearly to assessors and shared with students.*

Classroom Assessment for Teachers

Whether evidence for assessment is gathered during learning or generated using an assessment task, the way in which it is judged or marked has a significant impact on assessment validity and reliability. Instructions for judging or marking evidence should be aligned with the purpose and focus of the assessment and exactly match what students have been asked to do in an assessment task or during learning. They should be created at the same time as any task for students, or before, and ideally before evidence is gathered during learning. The way in which evidence for assessment is marked or judged and quality assured is important for assessment reliability and validity. It should be shared with students as well as assessors.

Chapter 10: Making good use of the outcomes of assessment

> *Practical Step 7:*
> *Present and use assessment outcomes for the purpose for which they were intended and in ways that maximise positive impacts on students and minimize negative ones.*

Different forms of assessment outcomes suit different purposes. They should be used for the intended formative and summative purposes in ways that maximise benefits and minimise harms to learning and student wellbeing. Having a clear understanding of what assessment outcomes can and cannot tell us will allow us to communicate and use these in appropriate ways. No matter how good assessment is in other ways, if the outcomes are used inappropriately the validity of that assessment will be undermined.

Appendix 1 is a diagram that shows how using these seven practical steps for good assessment can help create a clear line of thought from why and what and who you want to assess through every decision in

Overview of the principles of assessment and practical steps

the process of devising ethical assessment that is valid, reliable, fair and practical.

Appendix 1: The importance of alignment

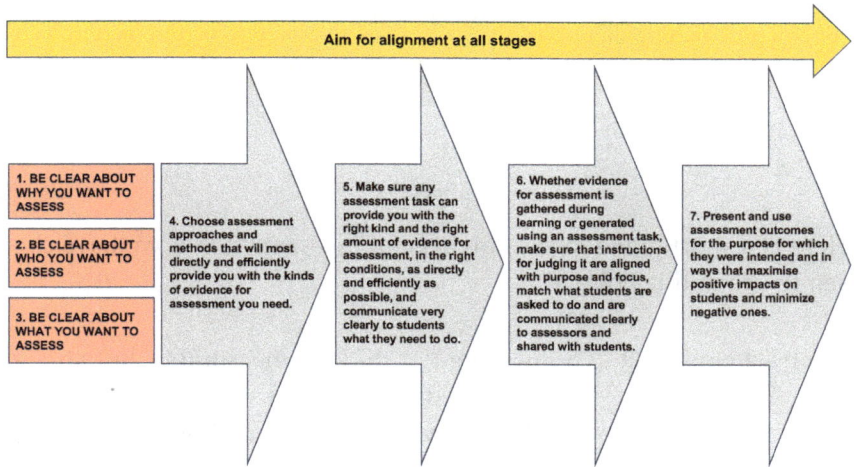

Glossary

Here is a short guide to the language of assessment that we have chosen to use in this book.

Abstract construct Something not directly measurable, but able to be described. Length and weight can be measured directly. Knowledge and skills, resilience and creativity cannot be measured directly, but they can be measured if we have a common understanding of what they *are* and what evidence of them would look like.

Assessment purpose The use to which assessment outcomes are intended to be put.

Assessment method Categories into which fit a range of types of assessment task according to common features and that offer different ways to assess different kinds of knowledge and skills. Examples of assessment methods are performance, examination, project and simulation.

Assessment task A set of instructions or questions (assessment items) that tell the student what to do, designed to help the student to provide relevant evidence for assessment.

Glossary

Assessment item	A discrete part of an assessment task. Examples of assessment items would include a multiple-choice question, an invitation to explain something in writing or orally, a matching task or a case study.
Assessor	Someone responsible for administering an assessment and/or judging the evidence for assessment.
Command verb	Verbs that are used in assessment tasks and items to tell students exactly what they need to do.
Competence-based assessment	Assessment that is focused on what is expected of the student, defined in a set of criteria.
Diagnostic assessment	Assessment used before learning to inform decisions about appropriate course placement and during learning to identify specific learning difficulties. Usually developed and tested by those with particular expertise and access to appropriate data.
Educational assessment	A process that involves the judging of evidence of learning and using the outcomes of that in a purposeful way.
Fair assessment	Assessment in which students are given equitable opportunities to demonstrate what they know and can do.
Formal assessment	Assessment carried out in a carefully planned and executed way, usually because the consequences of the assessment are especially important.
Formative assessment	A shorthand term for assessment for formative purposes, which is assessment primarily used to inform next steps in teaching and learning.

Glossary

High-stakes assessment	Assessment of which the consequences or 'stakes' are high.
Intended learning outcomes	Statements that clearly describe the knowledge and skills that students are expected to be able to demonstrate at the end of a course or period of learning.
Moderation	A process used after assessment has taken place to check that judgements on evidence for assessment have been made appropriately and consistently.
Observation	A method of assessment in which an assessor observes a student in the course of learning or while engaging with assessment tasks.
Outcomes of assessment	What is available for use at the end of the process of assessment. Outcomes of assessment should be designed for particular uses, and the forms they take would include written or verbal comments, marks or grades. Sometimes called 'results', especially in the case of assessment for summative purposes.
Practicality	The extent to which an assessment is manageable for student and assessor.
Reliability	The extent to which assessment is not influenced by a particular assessor or anything other than what it is intended to assess.
Quality assurance	Any means by which teachers or other assessment professionals ensure or improve the quality of assessment.
Question	Something that is asked using an interrogative sentence.
Standard	Criteria for success.

Glossary

Standardisation   A process designed to ensure a shared understanding and consistent application of criteria for judging evidence for assessment. This will often include **moderation** of assessment (see entry).

Student   Someone following a course of study at school, college, university, place of employment or other place of learning.

Summative assessment   A shorthand term for assessment for summative purposes, which is assessment primarily used to record past learning in summary form.

Validity   The extent to which an assessment really is measuring what it is intended to measure. This is established during the creation of an assessment and is the most important quality of any assessment.

Index

Note: Page numbers in **bold** indicate tables in the text

abstract constructs assessment 66–9
access arrangements 31
action verbs 65–6
alignment: in educational assessment 46, 87, 100–1, 106–9, 115, 134, 139
artificial intelligence (AI) 10
assessment 7–15; abstract constructs 66–9; approaches 74–6; conditions of 102–4; context for 101–2; drift 100–1; dyslexia 15, 30, 55–6; efficiency in 104–5; measurement and 8; for national qualifications 15, 29; origins 8–9; quality assurance of 119; *see also specific entries*
assessment for learning *see* formative assessment
assessment item 81, 88, 137; choice of 93; command verbs 94–5; communication 94; contexts in 95–6; extended response 91–3; generating evidence for assessment 87–8, 91–3; illustrations in 97; multiple-choice item 89; objective-type item 88–91; optional 98; scaffolding 99–100; short-answer item 90–1, 92; types 87–93
assessment of learning *see* summative assessment

assessment purpose 14, 19, 45, 46, 135; diagnostic 55–6; fitness for 35; formative (*see* formative assessment); judging of evidence and 111–12, **113–14**; and outcomes 121–2, 124–9; practicality and 34; reliability and 27–8; summative (*see* summative assessment); validity and 23–4
assessment systems 77, 81, 83
assessment task 137; clarity 25; command verbs 94–5; communication 94; context in 95–6; generating evidence for assessment 3, 11–12, 75–6, 87–8, 91–3; illustrations in 97; job of 75–76, 87, 94; optional 98; scaffolding 99–100; washback effect 87
assessor 3, 33, 77, 81, 106, 111, 118
assignment 78
aural test 79
authentic assessment 79–80

benefits: of educational assessment 38; maximising 40–2
bias(ed) 26, 41; *see also* fairness

case study 78, 81
cognitive skills assessment 76, 89, 92

Index

collaborative approach 67
command verbs 94–5
comments: assessment outcomes 123, 125–6; feed-forward 126; on strengths and weaknesses 123; *see also* feedback
communication: assessment outcomes 122, 125, 127, 129–31; assessment task/item 94; clarity 65, 94, 97, 105; judging of evidence 118
competence-based assessments 9, 34
conditions of assessment 102–4
consequences (assessment) 13–14, **14**, **19**, 37; negative 39–40; positive 37, 38, 41; *see also* outcomes of assessment
contexts: for assessment 101–2; in assessment tasks and items 95–6
creativity assessment 66–8
curriculum 10, 64, 69

deep learning 83, 128
diagnostic assessment 47, 48, 55–6, 129
digital assessments 10
discrimination 28–9, 40, 59; *see also* fairness
dissertation 78
dyslexia 15, 30, 55–6

educational assessment 1–2, 133; benefits and risks of 38–40; choice of 16; origins of 8–10; purpose, consequences, timing, frequency and formality of 13–14, **14**, **19**
ethical issues 41
ethics: of educational assessment 40–2, 104; medical 40
evidence for assessment 11–13, 136; adequacy 73–4; assessment task/item 87–8, 91–3; gathering 74; generating 3, 11, 12, 75–6, 104; nature of 75; observation 74; relevance 73–4; right kind/amount of 104, 105; tangible/ephemeral 11–12; *see also* assessment task; judgement; judging of evidence; method of assessment
examination 9, 79, 80–4
expert-devised diagnostic assessment 15
extended response items 91–3

fairness in educational assessment 28–32, 134; and inclusion 31–2, 59–61, 135; practicality and 33–4; unfairness and 30; validity and reliability and 29–30
feedback 17; effective 126; formative assessment 47, 49–50, 125–7
feed-forward commentary 126
focus of assessment 63–4; discussion with colleagues 69; shared with students 69–70; validity 63
formality of assessment 14, **14**, **19**
formative assessment 18, 47, 48–50, 135; effective 49, 50; features of 50; feedback 49–50, 125–7; frequency 48, 49; outcomes 47, 49–50, 121–2, 125–7; purpose of 48–50; summative *vs.* 47–8, 54
frequency of assessment 13–14, **14**, **19**

grades/grading 117–18; assessment outcome and 124, 128–31; overfocus on 128

high-stakes assessment 52–3, 96, 130

illustrations 97
inclusive assessment 31–2, 59–61, 135
informal approach 16–18
instructions: for judging evidence 107, 109; marking 110–16
intended learning outcomes 64–5; action verbs 65–6
international assessments 15
investigation 78

judgement/judging of evidence 3, 11–13, 16–17, 137-8; alignment 106–9, 115; allocating marks 116–17; assessment purpose 111–12, **113–14**; communication 118; grades 117–18; instructions for 107, 109; marking instructions 110–16; quality assurance 119; student's awareness 110

knowledge assessment 76–9, 81–2, 88–91

Index

language of assessment 2, 65, 77, 94–5

marks/marking: allocation 116–17; assessment outcome and 124, 117–18, 128–31; instructions 110–16
measurement 7–8
method of assessment 136; choice of 76–79, 85; exams 79, 80–4; oral 77; performance 78; portfolio 78–9; practical 78, 83; project 78; strengths and weaknesses 84–5; tests 79, 80–4; using more than one method 79
misleading 23, 39
moderation 53, 118, 119
multiple-choice items 89

objective-type assessment items 88–91
observation 17, 59, 74
opportunity/opportunities for students 1; assessment outcome 38; equitable 30–2, 59–60
optional tasks/items 98
oral assessment 77, 90
outcomes of assessment 3, 11, 17, 38, 40, 45, 47, 131; 138–9; cognitive impacts 127; comments 123, 125–6; communication 121–3, 125, 127, 129–31; diagnostic purposes 129; fair assessment 29; formative purposes 47, 49–50, 121–2, 125–7; forms of 122–4, 130; grades 123–4, 128–9; meaningful 130; reliable assessment 26; sharing 122, 127; summative purposes 47, 52–3, 121–3, 127–30; of valid assessment 23

pedagogy 10
peer discussion 126–7
pen and paper test 81
performance assessment 77, 78
poorly devised assessment 39
portfolio assessment 78–9
practical assessment 78, 83
practicality 32–3, 134; and assessment purpose 34; fairness, reliability and validity 33–4; lack of 33, 34
project-based assessment 78
purpose *see* assessment purpose

quality assurance 119
question(ing) 74, 76; evidence of knowledge 81–2; multiple-choice 89; oral 77, 82

reasonable adjustments 31
reliability 25–8, 134; and assessment purpose 27–8; fairness, validity and 29–30; judging evidence 118; practicality and 33–4; summative assessment 28; and validity 27–8
report(ing): end-of-term 18; to parents 47, 52, 53; summative assessment 52, 53
research project 78
resilience 66–7
resources 102
risks, minimising 40–2
rote learning 83, 128

sampling 82
scaffolding 99–100
short-answer items 90–1, 92
special arrangements 31
staged tasks/items *see* scaffolding
standardised assessments 16, 52, 117
standards-based assessment 116, 123, 124
stress 29, 39, 84
student(s): assessment focus 69–70; comments to 123, 125–6; communication 94, 97, 105; comparison 126; confusions 95–6, 105; educational assessment impacts on 37–40; engagement 37, 49, 69, 80, 122, 126, 127; feedback 17, 47, 49–50, 125–7; impact on learning 37, 69, 87, 122, 123, 125–7; knowing how you will judge their evidence 110; as partners 70; peer discussion 126–7; progress 39, 47, 53; target 58–9, 135; teacher-student interactions 17, 77, 126; wellbeing 39, 40; *see also* opportunities for students
subject experts 69
summative assessment 18, 47, 48, 51–5, 102, 135; formative *vs.* 47–8, 54; frequency 51; outcomes 52–3, 121–4, 128–9; purpose of 51–5; reliability 28; reporting 52, 53

Index

target students 58–9, 135–6
teacher(s) 3; authentic assessments 80; observing students 17; role 8, 15–16, 56; teacher-devised assessment 1, 3, 16–18, 81, 133; teacher-student interactions 17, 77, 126; washback effects 87
tests 79, 80–4
time pressure 102–3
timing 13–14, **14, 19**

unfair assessment 29–30, 39, 41, 93, 100, 102–3, 115; *see also* bias(ed); discrimination

validity 22–4, 94, 118, 134; assessment focus and 63; and assessment purpose 23–4; fairness, reliability and 29–30; lack of 23; marking and 116–17; practicality and 33–4; prioritizing 24; reliability and 27

washback effect 87
word limit 103
workplace assessment 77, 78, 101
written test 28, 79, 82–3, 115; *see also* pen and paper test

147

For Product Safety Concerns and Information please contact our EU representative GPSR@taylorandfrancis.com
Taylor & Francis Verlag GmbH, Kaufingerstraße 24, 80331 München, Germany

www.ingramcontent.com/pod-product-compliance
Lightning Source LLC
Chambersburg PA
CBHW071743150426
43191CB00010B/1669